Tea Time of Life

Enjoy!

With Love
Ethel S. Freeman

Tea Time of Life

A Second Collection of
Recipes and Reflections

Ethel S. Tucker

authorHOUSE®

AuthorHouse™
1663 Liberty Drive
Bloomington, IN 47403
www.authorhouse.com
Phone: 1-800-839-8640

First published by AuthorHouse   10/29/2011

ISBN: 978-1-4670-4053-2 (sc)
ISBN: 978-1-4670-4050-1 (hc)
ISBN: 978-1-4670-4052-5 (ebk)

Library of Congress Control Number: 2011917221

Printed in the United States of America

More than 2,000 copies of Author Ethel S. Tucker's first cookbook
"From Pilot Knob to Main Street: A Collection of Recipes from
Yesterday, Today and Tomorrow," were sold after it was published
in 2005. Receiving a signed copy of the cookbook during a
reception in Tucker's home is Louise "Tootsie" Hamilton.

About the Title

Ever since I wrote "From Pilot Knob to Main Street" in 2005, I've felt that I needed to write another book that would finish some stories and have recipes that I did not include in the first.

During a Sunday evening service at the Marion United Methodist Church, our wonderful pastor, Reverend Wayne Garvey, talked about the "Evening Time of Life." I was by far the oldest person there, and as I left and shook his hand I said, "I'm definitely in the evening time of life." He said, "Oh no Ethel, you are just in the 'Tea Time of Life.'" That sparked a cog in my brain—thus the title. Then my goal was to have the book ready for the printers by my 90th birthday on November 29, 2007. Due to my busy lifestyle my plans did not happen. So my goal then was to have it completed by my 92nd birthday on November 29, 2009. This year, I will celebrate my 94th birthday. To be in the "Tea Time of Life" is when we enjoy reminiscing and telling stories of our younger years.

After many Sunday dinners when I have nephews and families, Reverend Garvey and sometimes another friend or two for dinner, I tell them stories about how it was when I was growing up or some other topic they seem to enjoy. So I'm attempting to tell what I remember from when I was growing up.

Ethel S. Tucker

My Prayer of Thanks

Dear Lord:

Thank you for bringing me into this big, beautiful universe in the early part of the most eventful 20th century. The century when we witnessed the transition from horse-drawn transportation to space travel.

And LORD, thank you for giving me the health, the desire, the mind, and the guidance to share my remembrances with the generations, both present and future.

And LORD, I pray that you will give me the wisdom and ability to witness for you for the remainder of my time on Earth.

And LORD, I thank you for my family and my friends who have encouraged me on, and helped me in so many ways, especially after the death of my husband, Thomas N. Tucker.

In your precious name I pray,

Amen.

Foreword

Ethel Tucker is an anomaly. At 94, her flair for entertaining is unmatched in Marion, where she prepares elaborate teas and large dinners for family and friends. Quite certainly, she is among the few her age in the United States who polishes her best silver, pulls out her best china and puts on her best attire—including high heels—to host guests nearly every week of the year. During December 2010, just after celebrating her 93rd birthday, Tucker hosted 92 guests at multiple gatherings. Some were participants in a church-wide Christmas tea for United Methodist women; some were members of her fellowship circle at the Marion United Methodist Church; and the balance attended various dinners she prepared during the holiday season. Tucker grew up in an era before the invention of styrofoam plates, cake mixes and frozen entrees. She learned to cook on the staples from her family's or neighbor's orchard and garden. Despite many modern conveniences, Tucker sticks to her roots and graciously prepares made-from-scratch meals in her Marion kitchen for her minister, nephews and other close friends.

Her style is unmatched, especially for someone her age. Rarely are guests seated at her small kitchen table; instead, they are placed around her formal dining room table, which is exquisitely set for a full-course meal. To raise money for the historic community building where she graduated high school, a formal dinner at Tucker's home brought $1,000 during a 2009 auction.

She is an example to many, an inspiration to all. The younger generation considers it a treat to witness Tucker's elaborate style and amazing presentation.

By Allison Mick-Evans

* * *

The following perfectly illustrates Ethel Tucker's place as the matriarch of Marion and the cornerstone of her family, as written by her nephew, Alan Stout.

"We are going to Aunt Ethel and Uncle Tom's for dinner tonight." With those words from mom, I knew my brother Keith and I would be putting on ties and "dressing up" for dinner at Aunt Ethel's.

We would usually be seated in the sun room with Bill and Bohn Frazer, our cousins-in-law. Keith and I are the sons of the late Howard and Imogene Stout, and Bill and Bohn are the sons of the late Bob and Dorothy Frazer (sister of Thomas Tucker). Uncle Tom passed away in 2001. He was generally regarded as the foremost Crittenden County historian. Aunt Ethel is often referred to as the matriarch of our community.

Even as I have grown older, I have come to realize how special meal time at Aunt Ethel's is. On Wednesdays, we often gather there as well as for Sunday dinner after church. Aunt Ethel's table has also been a popular lunch spot for local attorneys and judges on "court day".

From the simplest lunch to the most extravagant dinner party, the food is always delicious and the presentation is always enticing. To this day, the most coveted dinner reservation in our community is a dinner party invitation at Aunt Ethel's.

This book is not just a recipe book. It tells the story of living in a small town and explores the fellowship developed when we break bread together.

Thanks to Aunt Ethel for all she has done.

By Alan C. Stout

Table of Contents

Mary Elizabeth Ridings Stout

Burton Benson Stout and his bride Mary Elizabeth Ridings, wearing the dress she made for the couple's wedding on September 27, 1906.

Tribute to my Mother

The Stout family was well established on Pilot Knob in the central part of Crittenden County. My father, Burton Benson Stout, married my mother, Mary Elizabeth Ridings, in 1906 and they settled on the farm that Burt and his father already owned. Burt and Lizzie had three children; Rosa Lee born in 1913, myself born in 1917, and Howard in 1919. In 1926, Burt died suddenly.

Mother was a Christian woman who asked God for guidance. Now she was a young widow with three children to raise. I can see her now on that August day in 1926, when she came to Marion wearing her black satin dress and a long black veil, riding in our new black Model T Ford that was only a few months old, with Charlie Conger driving her. That was the first of several trips she had to make to Marion to settle the estate. On those trips she also began thinking of moving to town to get us children in school. Before her marriage, she was a milliner in her hometown of Erin, Tennessee. But she seemed out of practice for such now after having been a farm wife and raising children for 20 years and loving every minute of it.

This rare Stout family photo was taken in Mr. Travis' studio in about 1922. Burton Benson and Mary Elizabeth Ridings Stout with children (from left) Howard, Ethel and Rosa Lee.

This photo of Ethel Stout, Rosa Lee Stout and Howard Stout and was taken in about 1936 at the family's home on Mound Park Avenue in Marion.

On one trip she talked with Mr. and Mrs. Stone, long time friends, about her problems. She decided to rent out the farm and move us to town. Mr. Stone owned some rental properties, so when one became vacant, she rented it and we began a hasty move to Marion in order to get us in school that fall. Rosa Lee was 13 and ready for high school, Howard had just turned 6 and was ready to start school, and I was ready for 4th grade.

In those times there were no widows' and children's government benefits as we have today. Mother was used to having meat in the smokehouse and canned goods in the cellar, so the move to town was a big adjustment. Mother's first job was selling Avon cosmetics door to door. This was a new market for Marion, as well as a new career for this young country widow-moved-to-town. As we studied our lessons at night Mother would be studying the information on Avon products. During the day she walked all over town calling on housewives to sell cosmetics. The interesting part of this to me now is that Mother never used any cosmetics except face powder as long as she lived.

Rosa Lee finished high school and went to teacher's college, at Mother's insistence, when she really wanted to take nurse's training. After she had taught two years, she made Mother give in and send her to nursing school at Deaconess Hospital in Evansville, Indiana. Rosa Lee became a surgical nurse and loved it. After working in Evansville a few years she and another nurse decided to go to California. They found suitable jobs in a hospital in Ft. Bragg, California. Both girls enjoyed the area, and they both married and raised families there. Rosa Lee died in 1967 and was buried alongside her husband, Ralph Pedersen, in a Ft. Bragg cemetery.

Howard Stout in Sicily, Italy during World War II

Although he was a popular cheerleader and teachers' pet, Howard did not like school. He liked to work and make things. However, Mother made him stay in high school four years, although he did not have enough credits to graduate. He first worked for Phillips Construction, and then went into the spar mining business. He enlisted early in World War II into the Army. He spent most of his time in the European Theater. He had married his first love, Imogene Crider, before the war in 1939. Mother and I lived together and worked together after Howard went to war, and we were naturally close.

In spite of all the hardships and heartaches, Mother was able to work, make a living, and raise three children that (I hope) were worthwhile contributions to society and always knew right from wrong. As the last survivor I'm so thankful for the faithfulness of my mother and want to be more like her.

As I'm getting into the "Tea Time of Life," I look back over almost a century that I've lived; it is only natural to think and reminisce about my personal accomplishments, pleasures, and hardships.

If you are interested in purchasing copies of
Tea Time of Life, contact Ethel S. Tucker at:

319 S. Main Street
Marion, KY 42064
(270) 965-4055

Acknowledgements

Alan and Doris Stout
Keith and Julie Stout
Bill and Sherry Frazer
Sara Frazer Taylor
Tara Blazina
Casey Knox
Emily Myers
Helen Moore
Helen Springs
Rev. Wayne Garvey
Allison Evans
Katie Cunningham
Brian Hunt

Chapter 1

Growing Up in the Great Depression:
Stories of Business, Entertainment & Travel

After Papa died and we moved to town, we still walked to school, walked home for lunch unless the weather was bad, in which case we would carry our lunch from home. People walked to work and to church until the automobile came on the market and people could afford to buy one.

For our school picnics we would walk the railroad tracks to Winlow Park, the most popular picnic spot.

I graduated from Marion High School in 1935. It was so exciting to walk across the stage at Fohs Hall to receive my diploma. Fohs Hall was less than 10 years old and was the new civic center that had been built by Julius Fohs and given to the community as a gift. Mr. Fohs had lived and gone to school in Marion. He went on to get his higher education and become a world renowned geologist. Mr. Fohs then wanted to do something for Marion in memory of his parents and where he grew up so this fine building was his decision. It is still in use today and is used for what it was intended.

As I talk with young family members about the differences of growing up during the Great Depression years and the present affluent, extravagant times today, they can hardly believe the contrasts. We did not have televisions, movie theaters, or automobiles. Radios became available by my teenage years. We walked to school, for there were no school buses, and we walked home for lunch for there was no cafeteria at school.

Growing Up in the Depression

Beginning at age 12 and throughout high school, I worked on Saturdays at Stone's Dry Goods and Variety Store. My mother worked in the store at the time. After graduation, I attended Bethel College in McKenzie, Tennessee. I lived in the Virginia Hotel that my Aunt Rosa Rushing, my mother's sister, owned and operated. I worked cleaning rooms in exchange for my room and board and walked the railroad tracks to Bethel College each day. When I returned from that one year of college, Mr. Stone asked me if I liked college and wanted to go back. I told him that I would rather work than continue my plans to be a teacher. So he hired me. Soon his health began to decline and he and his wife gave me half interest in the store. I became the buyer and manager. From late 1936-1943, I ran the store and Mother was the main clerk. Everything was very cheap, as well as wages.

Mr. and Mrs. Brooks Towns were salesmen who sold merchandise to local stores. In about 1938 they took Ruth McDaniel from Salem and me to the market in Indianapolis to buy Christian merchandise for our stores.

When business improved, the store bought a manual cash register to replace the money drawer. We did not have an adding machine to total the sales. We used our own brain and scratch pad to make sales tickets.

We had two widths of brown wrapping paper and a big cone of twine to wrap up the sales. Later, sacks became available.

We received our shipments of merchandise by train. A drayman, a man with a small wagon and horse, would bring it from the train to the store for $1.50 a load. Some merchandise became hard to get during World War II. One that I particularly remember was silk hose. When nylon came on the market, we could hardly get silk hose.

We sold a lot of fabrics. Most people made their own clothes for the family or had a dressmaker make them. In addition to fabric, we sold notions, underwear, shoes, and men's overalls, and we were the first female dry goods merchant in town. There were two ladies 'ready-to-wear' stores: Moore and Pickens in the old hotel building on East Carlisle Street and Lottie Terry's business on West Bellville Street. There was one other store that sold dry goods and men's ready-to-wear, that was Yandell and Gugenheim. That store was later purchased by Taylor and Vaughan. At Stone's Dry Goods and Variety Store, we rented one corner in the back of the store to two ladies, Maude Hughes and Ellen Nunn, for a sewing shop.

We rented the other back corner to Mr. Lindzey Crider for a shoe repair shop. He paid rent by sweeping floors and the front sidewalk, carrying in coal, and keeping the fire in the coal stove that heated the store. Both of these shops brought more traffic through our store and many times added to our sales.

Many times someone would see a pattern of fabric they liked so they would talk to Mrs. Hughes about making a dress. So we would make a sale of fabric and trimming, and Mrs. Hughes would get the money (about $3 for a cotton dress).

The shoe repair business was good too, as people walked and wore the soles and taps off their shoes. Most every pair of shoes we sold in the store would have at least one sole and heel repair and usually they would have two repairs.

Mary Elizabeth Ridings Stout stands beside Ethel and Howard's first car. This picture was taken the day Ethel Stout, Howard Stout, Imogene Crider, Jesse Maddux and Louis Maddux embarked on a trip to California to visit Rosa Lee Stout.

Our First Car

My brother Howard and I worked from about the time we were 12 years old. He mowed yards and worked in an ice cream shop. In 1937, we pooled our money and bought a '37 Chevrolet for about $275. He already knew how to drive, so he taught me. One Sunday afternoon he took me out on the newly graveled Shady Grove Road. He had me take the wheel and I drove! He would have me stop and start on a hill . . . you can see there was little or no traffic. We went to Deanwood and I circled the drive in front of the store and drove back to town. He told me that the next Sunday we would go again and he would teach me to back up and turn around. Well, the next Saturday night my mother and I closed our store at 9 p.m. Two girls, my cousin Gertrude Stout and a friend, Marshall Lee Green, were loafing in the store. I got the idea to take them for a drive. I went two doors up the street to where Howard was working in the ice cream parlor and I told him I was going to take Mother and the girls for a ride. We went on the same road that he had taught me on the Sunday before. The road was not as thickly populated as it is now. We went a very short distance and Mother said, "Honey, you better turn around." I just kept driving, for I did not know how to turn around! We went to Dean's store and I turned around in the same circle drive as I had done during my first driving lesson. The good Lord was with me. We had enough gas to get back to Marion just as Howard was getting off from work, so he took the girls home, and Mother, he, and I went home. As I told him where we went, he was pleased that I'd made it and he said, "Well we'll take another road for the next lesson." I think that was brotherly love. He was not upset with me. That was before the time of driver's licenses and driving tests.

Other Businesses in the 1930s and 1940s

Around the town square there were three drug stores, all of which had tables and chairs, fountain service, and two of them offered curb service. The more affluent women generally went to these in the afternoon for a Coke and a visit. There were also five grocery stores, two men's clothing stores, two hardware stores, one furniture and undertaking businesses, two banks, two poultry houses, two restaurants, two barber shops, a wholesale grocery business, a sewing shop and later a beauty salon.

As the automobile became popular, we had three garages that sold new cars and serviced them as well. We also had two filling stations as they were called. They sold gasoline for about 19¢ per gallon. The most popular station was where the Marathon station now sits at the corner of Main and Bellville streets.

If your date could afford a car, you usually rode on the new roads as they were built and then parked at the drug store for curb service, where you could see and be seen, and eat ice cream.

The grocery stores did not have fresh produce as we have today. They did have stalks of bananas hanging in the store windows. You could pick off as many as you wanted to buy. Usually you would get one or two ripe and the rest not so ripe.

There was also one butcher shop in Marion. You could get a soup bone with some meat on it for 10¢. A pound of unsliced bacon was 20-25¢.

Near the railroad station on the east side of town was an ice house and coal yard. Both the ice and coal came in by train. The ice man used a horse-drawn wagon to deliver house-to-house. The housewife would put a card in the window to tell the ice man how much ice to bring into the house. It came in 25-, 50-, 75-, or 100-pound blocks. Children would follow along as the ice man chipped the block of ice and would eat the ice that fell to the street.

There was a dairy at the edge of town. Mr. Elder owned it and delivered milk door-to-door in glass bottles. The housewife would put out as many clean empty bottles as she wanted replaced with milk and/or cream.

Winters

During the winters when it snowed, property owners were required to clean sidewalks within eight hours or they would be fined.

Times have changed so—now not many people walk and so many times in residential areas sidewalks aren't cleaned. The property owners are more likely to have a tractor with a blade hired to clean the driveway so they can get their cars out. This is another change that I can recognize.

Poultry Houses

People would go to Koltensky or W.E. Belt's poultry houses to buy their chickens, ducks, or turkeys.

I remember when mother wanted to get a chicken to fry we would go to the poultry house and buy a fryer for about 75¢. They would tie the chicken's feet together and we would walk home, taking turns carrying it. Every home had a chicken coop that you could put the chicken in for a few days if you thought it needed to fatten up.

Most every house in town also had a garden, and all members of the family helped hoe the garden.

Funeral Homes

In the early 1920s, Mr. Haynes and Mr. Taylor of Haynes & Taylor Drug Store got ice during the winter from a mine's lake and took to their store. Mr. Haynes' wife made ice cream and the men cranked the freezers and sold homemade ice cream in their drug store. My father-in-law, Mr. Ollie Tucker, was the pharmacist in that drug store in those years. Mr. Tucker later became an embalmer and had the funeral business along with a furniture store and partnered with W. H. Franklin. In the first quarter of the 1900s, most of the furniture, including coffins, was made by local craftsmen. The coffins were made of pine, covered on the outside with cloth. Black cloth was used for men's caskets and white or gray for women's.

There were no funeral homes as we know today. When someone died, the funeral director was called, and he would take his embalming supplies and a casket to the home. He would lay a plank that he brought with him between two kitchen chairs. This is where the terms "laid out" or "cooling boards" came from. He would put the body on this board and prepare it for burial. If the deceased lived very far from town he would spend the night, as the burial would be the next day. Neighbors would dig the grave in the neighborhood cemetery.

Starting a House

For a couple to start keeping house, the items needed were a table and chairs, cook stove, a bedstead and springs. The bride's family would usually furnish the featherbed from their extras. Featherbeds were made using a bed-size tick, or case, filled with duck, chicken, or turkey feathers. It was customary that the bride's parents gave the featherbed. The more affluent couple would also get a dresser and mirror and a rocking chair.

Beauty Parlors

One of the most appreciated businesses that actively started during the Depression in Marion was the beauty parlors. I do not remember who the very first permanent wave was given to in Marion, but this is the story told to me by Emily Shelby and I believe she got her information from Helen Moore. In the late 1920s Mildred Croft, a partner in the Moore and Pickens ready-to-wear store, went to Louisville to learn how to give a "little perm" on a tiny machine. The machine had two tiny rollers which could be used at the same time. The lady receiving the permanent was Mrs. Martha Lear Harpending. It took the whole day to give the permanent, two curlers at a time, and the charge was $5. Those who remember Mildred will remember that her patience would have soon been exhausted, so her permanent giving was very short lived.

The first permanent wave I got was about the time I was in high school and Neva Clement gave it to me in her shop, which was upstairs over Stone Dry Goods and Variety Store, which later became the Red Front Grocery. I don't remember what I paid, but I think $5 was the price back then.

Carrie Ainsworth opened up a very modern beauty parlor in one of the office spaces in the Woman's Club building. She went to Louisville and bought a Duret Perm Machine for $25 and gave permanents for $5, and charged 75¢ for a shampoo and set.

Another story told to me by Helen Moore is that her friend, a girl by the name of Stewart, begged her mother to let her get a perm at Carrie's Beauty Shop. Her mother finally gave in and so the girl got the perm, and when asked about it she said it was fine until she "poured embalming fluid on her head." The odor of early permanent waves was never very pleasing.

Soon beauty parlors were all over town and some in people's homes in the country. The names of the beauticians that I remember were Lillie Bradford, Bonnie Malcom, Grethel Vaughn, Evelyn McConnell, Corman Damron, Dee Dee Phillips, Hazel Springs, Polly Herrin, Rose York Stout, Irene Royce, Martha Kirk, Margie Belt, Shirly Enoch, Emily Shelby, Charlotte Fox, Russene Heaton, Sharon Riley, Sue Millikan, Jessica James, and Debbie Summers.

Emily Shelby started working at Debbie Phillips' shop when she first moved to Marion. She opened the Fashion Beauty Salon and Charlotte Fox worked with her. That salon closed in 2010.

Russene Heaton and Sharon Riley opened the Nu-U, now located on South Main Street, in 1987.

Barber Shops

Marion has usually accommodated at least two and sometimes three barber shops. I'm sure their customs and customers have changed through the years as well as the prices. I think when I was a very young girl, getting my hair cut with bangs was about 50¢. Names of barbers that I remember are Eugene Macky, Mason Daniels, Blanton Wiggins, Walter McConnell, Fred Mety, Rurie Winters, Noble McDaniel, Ronnie Bealmear, Ray Johnson, Lilly Cruce, Moze Mitchell and Mr. Herrell, Rex Brown, Clany McConnell, Paul Brown, Dickie Gough, and Jewell Penn. There are at present two barber shops, and the barbers are Mike Crabtree, Roy Rogers, and Tim Harrison.

Restaurants

Of all the restaurants, I can best remember Givens on Main Street in the Marvel building. They cooked and served the first corn sticks I ever saw. They used the old fashion cast iron stick pans. Guy and Minnie Givens ran the restaurant for years. Their son J.J. worked in the restaurant. They had a daughter, Delia, and she was a nurse who specialized in caring for babies. In later years she became an inventor. She borrowed $20 from Neil Guess and started her business selling infant wear and the item known as Dee's Half Pint, a child's urinal for parents to take in the car when small children traveled. She also made the first disposable diapers.

Crittenden Hotel

The Crittenden Hotel, which was located on East Carlisle Street, was the place to go for dinner in the 1930s and 40s. Mr. and Mrs. Albert Cannon ran it and had a dining room that accommodated the hotel guests and local people as well. I never ate there until after I married. When we came home on a weekend leave, Mr. and Mrs. Tucker would take the family for Sunday dinner. Times changed, and it ceased to be a hotel and became just a rooming house with stores on part of the first floor. Eventually the stores closed and the building was torn down. It was located where the Marion Baptist Church parking lot is today. Another change I can reminisce about.

Reverend James Boone in Piney Fork

While working on this book I talked with Reverend James Boone. He told me of his growing up in the Piney Fork community. At 100 years old, he still remembers the two grocery stores at Piney where eggs were 10¢ a dozen and coffee was sold in 25-pound packages.

8

He and his brother worked in tobacco and hauled it by wagon to Dycusburg where it was loaded on barges for shipment. He tells of leaving home at 3 a.m., and returning at about 10 at night.

Mr. Boone told me of other work including electrical work. When the Rural Electric came in, he wired houses from Marion to Smithland, his biggest wiring job being the Smithland Methodist Church.

About the Town and Entertainment

The streets were dirt with stepping stones at the main corners. During the summer they would oil the main streets to keep down the dust. When the women knew they would be crossing the freshly oiled streets they would put down newspapers to walk on so as not to get their shoes messed up.

The opera house was upstairs over the stores on the north side of Bellville Street. They presented live entertainment as well as showed silent movies before talkies came about. My husband Thomas told the story about his grandmother taking him to the silent movie and reading the script to him in a low voice, and he would fuss that he could not hear her.

Everyone looked forward to the Chautauqua (various traveling shows and local assemblies) that flourished in the United States in the late 19th century and early 20th century. They provided popular education combined with entertainment in the form of lectures, concerts, and plays. They were modeled after activities at the Chautauqua Institution of western New York, coming to town each summer for a week of shows, music, and lectures. They set up their big tent on what was then Jocky Lot (now the Farmers Bank parking lot). After they stopped coming, a smaller show called the Bisbee show came and set up on Poplar Street.

The Last Store to Leave

Around the courthouse square in about 2005, Hunt's Department Store closed and moved two blocks south to a newly remodeled store where it operates its existing trophy business. It is known as Superior Trophies and Screen Printing. This move ended a four-generation business in one location at the corner of Main and Bellville streets. R. C. Hamilton began working for his father-in-law, Hillis Hunt, in his store in 1944 under the G. I. Bill. He returned from his tour of duty and was paid to work and go to school through the federal on-the-job training program.

His son, Mike, grew up in the store, as did Mike's sister Patsy. Mike remained active in the store during his term of teaching school for 26 years. When he retired from teaching, he continued full time in the trophy and screen-printing business.

Marion's Oldest Businesses

Two prominent businesses of the mid-19th century still carry the torch in the community.

The Crittenden Press was founded in 1879 by R.C. Walker. Its success grew through the years as the newspaper was purchased several times during its first 100 years. In 1960, Evers Mick purchased the newspaper from Charles E. Pepper. Upon Evers Mick's death in 1969, his son Paul Mick began overseeing daily operations. The newspaper remains in the Mick family, with Allison Mick-Evans and her husband Chris Evans managing daily operations. The Press has kept up with the times and continues to be an outstanding weekly paper in Kentucky.

Henry & Henry Monuments began in 1881 by Rev. J.B. Henry in the back yard of his residence on West Bellville Street in Marion.

In 1906, a brother acquired a concrete building on East Carlisle Street and moved the business there, where it remained until 1949 when the company moved to its present location on Sturgis Road.

Henry & Henry has been in the Henry family continuously and is presently owned by Billy Fox, son of Joan Henry Fox and her husband Bill Fox. Billy is the fifth generation to manage the monument company.

County Fair

Another big event was the county fair. The first one I remember attending was north of town in an area known as Flynn's Field. It was about 1924, and I was about 5 years old and my sister, Rosa Lee, was about 10 years old. Our father took us to the fair while Mother stayed home with Howard. I ate my first hamburger at the fair. The American Legion and Auxiliary had been organized by the World War I veterans and wives, and its members fried hamburgers on a kerosene stove and sold them. I've liked hamburgers ever since then! I also remember that I saw an airplane for the first time. I think it was on display only.

The flood of 1937, as shown at Dam 50 on the Ohio River,
displaced many Crittenden Countians, destroyed many
homes and created quite a disruption for businesses.

The Flood of 1937

My mother had to be hospitalized in Evansville just before the waters
rose. My sister was a nurse at Deaconess Hospital and was looking after
Mother. But Howard and I were at home with Aunt Mollie who was
staying with us. The patients had to be evacuated. Mother and Rosa Lee
left Evansville on the last train for St. Louis (the only direction that tracks
were not under water).

The hospital found out from patients if they had relatives west of
Evansville. Mother had two brothers-in-law in St. Louis, so they were
notified when to meet the train to pick up my ailing mother and my sister.
They stayed more than a week before we knew where they were, since
telephone service was out.

We had a radio, which we listened to as much as possible. We heard
on the radio that some patients from Deaconess Hospital went to St.
Louis. We hoped that would be where Mother was. In a few days we
received a telegram from her and Rosa Lee that they were with the Stouts
and being well cared for. Marion was surrounded by water in all directions

except toward Princeton. Stranded refugees from Sturgis and Blackford were brought to Marion and housed in the Methodist Church and the First Baptist Church.

Government commodities were brought in to help feed them. Some church members prepared food at their homes as the Baptist Church did not have kitchen facilities.

I remember a story that my husband Thomas enjoyed telling. After the water receded, the refugees were taken home but they still came to Marion for their commodities. One old man from Webster County came for some groceries, and when they started to give him some grapefruit he said, "We won't take them. We tried to boil them and fry them and we just didn't like them. So we will leave them for someone else."

I have now lived through the second-worst flood in modern history. This April 2011, more than 13 inches of rain caused major flooding along the Ohio, Cumberland and Tradewater rivers. About 50 homes were evacuated in Tolu, Dycusburg and Weston. By the first of May, Marion was only accessible by one route, U.S. 641. Water covered 40 state and county roads, causing extreme travel difficulties for people in the area.

Life in the Depression

The Great Depression made the housewife more conscious about economy. She learned to save as never before. In fact, I believe that in spite of the hardships, those of us who grew up in the Depression years are stronger in many ways—physically, more knowledgeable about how to manage, and more appreciative of what we have. We grew up learning to take care of what we had and when it broke, to fix it . . . not tear it down and build a new one.

It was during the Depression years that casserole cooking was introduced in America. During the Depression, housewives used every method to feed the family as well as possible and as economically as possible.

Money was very scarce and at the same time the groceries and meats were in short supply in the stores. Sugar and coffee became rationed as well as gasoline, for those who were fortunate enough to have cars.

The radio was introduced in 1926, and the following year a national network was formed. The U.S. Department of Agriculture became interested in helping farmers market reports, and then came "Aunt

Sammy's," a 15-minute radio program every morning. She gave advice on what to feed the family for dinner, how to clean the house, how to fix leaks, how to make a dress, or how to raise both vegetables and babies. We didn't have a radio then, but I can only imagine how excited my mother would have been to have this advice on such matters. As it was, many homemakers, especially those in more rural areas, had to rely on trial and error when they encountered difficulties. The program lasted nearly 20 years, until 1944.

The Great Depression cookbook of Aunt Sammy's recipes was published during this time. The idea of casserole meals and one-dish meals was introduced. Everyone had to save whatever was left over and the next day add whatever was available and thus another meal would be served. Aunt Sammy planned her meals to be economical, practical, and good to eat. Several of my favorite casserole recipes from her book are in that section of this book. I have also included some modern casserole recipes that are an outcome of the Depression era. The current recipes have more ingredients, especially herbs and seasonings.

Thomas' Experience with the Great Depression

The most remembered time of the Depression was when the banks were closed that day in 1929. It was called the year of the crash.

My husband, Thomas Tucker, liked to tell this story: It was always a treat for him when his Uncle Clem Nunn would take him to Paducah for the day. Well this day Thomas had some spending money, but Uncle Clem didn't have any cash on hand and intended to get some cash at a bank in Paducah where he did part of his banking. Lo and behold, when they got to Uncle Clem's law office in Paducah, he heard the news that the banks were closed. Thomas had to pay for their lunches and Uncle Clem had to borrow whatever Thomas had for bridge fare on the return home. Thomas did not get to go to a movie that afternoon as he had planned.

Mt. Rushmore under construction

Jesse Maddux, Howard Stout and Lewis Maddux

Ethel Stout and Jesse Maddux at The Chandelier
Tree in the Redwood National Forest

Howard Stout, Ethel Stout and Imogene Crider packing for their trip

Imogene Crider and Howard Stout at the base of Mt. Rushmore

On the set of a film being shot in Hollywood

Our Famous Trip

By 1939, we decided to get some other young people who had worked and saved their money to go on a trip. Howard was madly in love with Imogene Crider—so she was the first one to ask. We were friends with Jesse and Louis Maddux from Salem. (They hung out at the ice cream parlor when they came to Marion.) So the five of us got together and planned a trip to California. Our parents were supportive of our trip. We decided we would visit our sister in northern California and then go down to San Francisco to the World's Fair. We figured we would spend $500 each. Since I was the oldest (I was 22, and they were 18-21 years old), I was made the treasurer of the group. Next, we had to consider how were we going to get luggage for five in the trunk. I'll never know how, but we did! Gasoline was about 19¢ a gallon and many of the highways were still gravel and poorly marked. We went a northern route and stopped at Mt. Rushmore, South Dakota, where they were chiseling on the presidents' visages by the sculptor, Gutzon Borglum. It was not completed until 1941 and was made into a national memorial. It is still a great tourist attraction today.

It took us a week to get to Ft. Bragg, California. After visiting Rosa Lee and Great Redwood, California, we went to San Francisco and took Rosa Lee with us. (That made six). We visited the Golden Gate Exposition in San Francisco. This was two years after the Golden Gate Bridge was completed in 1937. I don't remember much about the event, other than there were beautiful flowers everywhere and many fountains. I also remember a telephone company which had telephones set up and you could talk and hear yourself. Its purpose was to show people that they should speak distinctly when talking on the phone. Rosa Lee went on to Hollywood with us. This was a peak time for tourists. Rosa Lee went back to Ft. Bragg by bus from Los Angeles, and we started homeward along a southern route. When we hit the desert, we were advised at a gas station to buy a box of dry ice to put in one window and roll up all the others. You see, this was long before air-conditioned automobiles. Well, with five in the closed up car, I seemed to get short of air. So, we tossed the dry ice, rolled down the windows and took the hot wind. The boys all smoked, which added to the discomfort when we used dry ice. All in all a great time was had by all, and we got home with a few dollars each. I'd say that was a far cry from what could be done nearly 70 years later.

On the trip we usually stayed in tourist cottages. Usually one cottage would accommodate the five of us. These cottages were not very close together and were situated over the grounds around a filling station. Usually there was a restaurant on the grounds or a small grocery store where we would eat our supper. These tourist cottages were usually out in the country or on the outskirts of a town. Motels were not in existence yet—I suppose they were an outcome of the tourist cottages. The first and only tourist cottages in Crittenden County were at Winlow Park, east of Marion on U.S. 60. They were owned and operated by Mr. and Mrs. Virgil Stone. When we got to a larger city by evening time we would stay in a hotel. This trip was made before travel agencies or even road maps were popular. Therefore, every time we stopped at a filling station we would inquire how far it was to the next town and what things of interest could be seen in between.

World War II

By 1941, many of our young men were drafted for service in World War II. Some enlisted to avoid being drafted and by so doing they could have some choice in their duty. The first draftees left Marion by train. Many friends and families went to the depot to see them off. Later Mr. J.H. Orme started the bus agency and ran it from his drug store. The next draftees left by bus. Mr. Orme would watch to see the bus coming in sight and he would yell out, "By Jacks—Big Yellow Bus is here." Young wives, sisters, and friends would get together and make candy and cookies to send to the boys while they were still in training in the country.

Pearl Harbor

I remember December 7, 1941, the Pearl Harbor attack. We were at war! It was a Sunday late afternoon and my date was Gilbert Cloyd. We were sitting at a stop sign at the corner of Main and Bellville streets in his new Chevrolet that had a radio, when we heard the news.

It was also in 1941 that Irving Berlin's popular musical, "White Christmas," starring Bing Crosby was released. It has become an all-time holiday favorite.

Fluorspar

Fluorspar operations were another major means of livelihood in Crittenden County in the first half of this greatest century. Crittenden County, Kentucky and Hardin County, Illinois were the fluorspar capitals of the world in the 1920s, 30s, and most of the 1940s. The revenue that the mines brought into this county helped us to overcome the Depression. Big name mining operations such as U.S. Steel set up mines in Crittenden County. All was well until they all had to pull out and go to Mexico where fluorspar could be mined at a lower cost because of cheaper labor.

Our Marriage

In 1943, Thomas Tucker and I were married. He served in the Navy as a pharmacist and was on a new hospital ship, The USS Sanctuary, until the war ended in 1945. His tour of duty started at the Great Lakes for training. We married while he was stationed there. Soon after our marriage, Mr. Stone and I sold the inventory of the Dry Goods & Variety Store that we had owned for several years. I then joined Thomas at Great Lakes where we were fortunate to get an efficiency apartment in Waukegan, Illinois. The hospital ship he served on went to Nagasaki, Japan and picked up patients who survived the atomic bomb and took them to a distribution center in Okinawa.

When Thomas returned home he joined the family business. His father died in 1947, his father's partner, W.H. Franklin, in 1949, and his mother in 1951. Thomas purchased the other half of the business and became the sole owner of the funeral business as well as the furniture business.

Gwendolyn Matthews at work at Tucker Interiors

Employees and spouses of Tucker Funeral Home & Tucker
Interiors, circa. 1950. Seated, Gladys Taylor and Alford Moore;
(standing) Myrtle Andrews, Bob Crooks, Larry Davidson, Thomas
Tucker, seamstress Gwendolyn Matthews and Ethel Tucker.

Tucker Funeral Home & Tucker Interiors, circa. 1970.

Ethel Tucker during the 1970 opening of Tucker
Interiors above Tucker Funeral Chapel.

Ethel and Thomas Tucker at the 1970 opening of Tucker Funeral Chapel on West Bellville Street in Marion.

A business we decided would go well with the furniture store was home decorating. So in 1954-1955, I studied home decorating and graduated from New York School of Interior Design. The business, which was in the upstairs of the funeral home, grew quickly. Gwendolyn Matthews was a faithful seamstress who made some beautiful curtains and draperies that are still in use in some of the homes in our area. As the business grew, we hired Sharon Belt Henshaw who became an expert upholsterer and seamstress. My great-niece and nephew had great fun using the carpet samples to ride down the long flight of stairs. I kept the decorating shop until my retirement in 1982.

In the years after World War II, the ways of doing business changed very quickly. We used our home, which was one block from town, for a funeral home for about 20 years. In 1970, we sold the furniture and appliance business to Johnson's and turned the whole building into a modern funeral chapel facility. In 1982, Thomas reached retirement age and had a chance to sell the business to the local competitor, Mr. Terry Gilbert, who still operates the Gilbert Funeral Home with his sons.

Modern Developments

By the end of the century, healthcare providers and hospitals were in every town, even the smallest ones. Marion's first hospital was opened in 1944, in what was built for a residence by the affluent Hayward family on North Walker Street. It was also used by the Board of Education for approximately 25 years as Marion High School. By 1972, a bigger and better hospital was needed, so the new building was built on U.S. 60 West, and is still in use today, after several expansions and upgrades.

By the last quarter of this century, the Crittenden County Convalescent Center was built, as was the Family Practice Clinic. During this same time the county built its first public library. Mrs. Jessie Croft Ellis, who was born in Marion and lived her early life here, returned when she retired in Michigan and got the first public library started in an empty store building. As times changed more, government aid was available and finally a fine modern public library was built. After Mrs. Ellis' health forced her to retire again, Margaret Waters Rhem became the librarian.

I saw factories establish themselves in Marion. Moore Business Forms was the first and then Potter & Brumfield—then several have come—some stayed, some left.

Ethel Stout graduated in 1935 from Marion High School at Fohs Hall. The building is now Marion's community center. Painting by Nicky Porter.

Between 1981-1997, I served as the resident director of Fohs Hall Community Arts Foundation. I enjoyed serving my community and helping to organize cultural events in Fohs Hall, the same building where I graduated high school. When I retired, I was honored with a painting of myself created by local artist Nicky Porter. It hangs in the Nunn Room today. At age 94, I am active on the board of directors and assist with events at Fohs Hall, and take care of reservations for the building, which is rented for wedding receptions, birthday celebrations and class reunions.

Events/Changes I can remember

In 1930-1931, Scotch tape was invented, and foam rubber, electric razors, and Alka Seltzer were developed.

In 1932, the Empire State Building opened as the world's tallest building. The crime of the century was that the Lindbergh baby was kidnapped.

In 1933, the Parker Brothers invented Monopoly, the world's best selling board game.

By World War II, DuPont had introduced nylon. It was used for making parachutes and hose fabrics to name a few items.

In 1936, the first vitamin pills were marketed in the United States.

In 1937, the Golden Gate Bridge was opened in San Francisco. Mother was visiting San Francisco at the time for the birth of her first grandson.

In 1940, the Jeep, a general purpose four-wheel drive vehicle was adopted by the American armed forces. During World War II my brother Howard used Jeeps for transportation when he was stationed in Europe. He always used Jeeps for his business when he returned to Kentucky after the war. His sons Keith and Alan inherited the love for the Jeeps as their adult toys.

After the war in 1947, the Polaroid camera was introduced. Microwave ovens were introduced in the United States, but not affordable for many homes for several years.

Velcro fasteners were invented in Switzerland in about 1950, but not introduced in the United States until much later. I used velcro in the decorating shop for valences and slip covers.

During the 1950s, television sets were in most homes. In order to see programs, you had to have a TV tower and antenna which cost as much as the television. Our boys at the shop had to learn how to install these and connect them to the televisions. When the families had saved enough money to buy the antenna and tower, they wanted them erected that day!

By 1954, frozen food sales topped $1 billion in the United States. Rock and Roll swept the United States along with crew cuts and Elvis Presley's "That's All Right Mama."

Lifestyle Changes

Through the years, many things have changed. I witnessed the evolution from baths being taken in the wash tub by the kitchen stove to the elaborate bathrooms in today's homes, many of which have three or four bathrooms. Things have changed from having one pair of shoes in the closet to a closet full; from the horse and buggy to the auto, to vans, to air and space travel as well. With all these changes, there is still the same amount of time! I can remember when people had time to sit on their porches or under the shade tree in their front yard, and they had time to invite a friend to stop and visit. We dare not stop and chat without first calling to see if they have time, yet there are still 24 hours in every day. I ask if modern technology has taken over? Even when I am shopping in a grocery and I see someone down the aisle that I haven't seen for some time and I look forward to a short chat, I often meet her in the aisle and realize she is engaged in deep conversation on her cell phone. She nods to me and I nod back to her!

I want you all to know that I love you just as Jesus loves me! He tells me in John 3:16, a verse I learned very young in the Card Class at Crooked Creek Baptist Church when my mother was the teacher, and I quote, "For God so loved the world that he gave his only begotten Son, and whoever believes in Him shall not perish but have everlasting life." It sustains me as many other teachings of the Bible from the Old and New Testaments, and I wish the same for all.

Family Genealogy

As this book is published near the finish of my long life, I want to name the nephews and families that have been a big part of my life, since I have outlived my husband Thomas, my sister, my brother, cousins, and many friends. I wonder if the nephews, when they are over four-score and thirteen years, will remember growing up in this age of the new millennium and will record their story of growing up in the greatest era for future generations. I wonder if they will have as many changes to record as I have had. Their genealogy follows.

Bill and Sherry Frazer

Bill Frazer, nephew—Bill was born December 31, 1945 to Robert and Dorothy Tucker Frazer. Sherry was born September 6, 1947, the daughter of Bruce and Daisy Wolterman-Weimer. Bill and Sherry Frazer were married July 16, 1966. They reside in Marion where Bill works in geology and mining. Sherry is a registered nurse who is raising grandchildren, coaching swimming and working in the community mineral museum. "My favorite thing to do is being with Aunt Ethel," Sherry said. "She is a wonderful, remarkable lady, aunt and best friend."

Ashley, Bohn, Jennifer and Linda Frazer

Bohn Frazer, nephew—Bohn Frazer is the son of the late Robert N. and Dorothy Tucker Frazer. Bohn graduated from Kentucky Military Institute in 1965. He then received a bachelor's degree from Hanover College in geology in 1969. Soon after, he was called to military duty where he served two years in the U.S. Army. After his discharge, he returned to college at the University of Missouri, Rolla where he received a bachelor's degree in mining engineering. He married Linda White, daughter of Robert L. and Ada Gahagen White on November 27, 1971. Linda received her undergraduate degree from the University of Kentucky and later a master's degree from Murray State. They have two daughters, Jennifer, who lives in Boulder, Colorado, and Ashley who lives in Clayton, Missouri. Through the years, Bohn worked for mining companies in several states. He retired in management from Americold Logistics in the Kansas City area. Bohn and Linda currently reside in Shawnee, Kansas, a suburb of Kansas City.

Burton and Dawn Pedersen

Burton Pedersen, nephew—Burton Pedersen is the son of Rosa Lee Stout Pedersen. Rosa Lee died in May 1967. Dawn and Burt were married November 14, 1964 in Eureka, California, the center of the Redwood Empire. Their plans to remain in the area were changed during the flood of 1964. In 1964, Burton started his 30-plus year career in the airline industry and was transferred immediately to Meford, Oregon. Dawn continued working in the banking industry. Burt's corporate position took him through various corporate mergers, and they were moved to San Francisco, Atlanta and finally to Phoenix, where they live in retirement. Burt has taken up golf and Dawn is very active in various quilting circles.

Alan and Doris Stout

Alan Crider Stout, nephew—Alan Crider Stout and Doris Jean Crider Guess were married on November 19, 1983 at the Marion United Methodist Church in Marion, Kentucky. Their marriage was officiated by Rev. Gainy Bohannon and Rev. Eugene Roberts. Doris is the daughter of James E. "Bud" Crider and Anna Katherine "Katie" Crider of Marion, Kentucky. Alan is the son of the late Howard P. Stout and Imogene Stout of Marion. They have three children, Erica Lynn Guess, Katherine Elizabeth "Katie" Cunningham and Logan Stout. Alan practiced law in Marion for 30 years. He also formed Stout, Farmer and King, a law firm in Paducah, Kentucky in 2000. He served five terms as Crittenden County Attorney from 1986-2006. He served on the Board of Regents of Murray State University from 2004-2010 and served as Chairman from 2007-2010. He has served on the Board of Directors of Farmers Bank and Trust Company since 2003. He served as Chapter 7 Bankruptcy trustee since 1986 and Doris was the manager of his Trustee operations. In 2011, Alan was selected for a 14-year term as U.S. Bankruptcy Judge for the Western District of Kentucky.

Keith and Julie Stout

Howard Keith Stout, nephew—Howard Keith Stout was born in 1949 to Howard and Imogene Crider Stout. Keith graduated in 1967 from Crittenden County High School and from Murray State University in 1972 where he was active in Alpha Tau Omega Fraternity. Keith ventured into the coal business straight out of college and continued until he closed the mines in 1981. He moved to Sarasota, Florida where he sold heavy equipment, ran an asphalt paving company, and then a sand and gravel business. Keith met Julie, a secretary for a construction and mining company in El Jobean, Florida. They married in January of 1986. They moved from Florida back to Crittenden County in 1990 where they lived on a farm they named Dog Days. Keith worked for Forke Brothers Auctioneers from 1990 until 1998. Keith continues to do heavy equipment appraisals and auctions. In 2010, the couple moved to Lake Barkley where they enjoy boating, Keith enjoys Jeeping and Julie enjoys horseback riding. They have one son, Jacob Selph, who is married to Jody Summers. Jacob and Jody have one daughter named Anna Marie.

Jennifer Frazer

Jennifer Frazer, great-niece—Jennifer is the first daughter of Bohn and Linda Frazer, born in Cleveland, Tennessee on July 28, 1978. Until she was about six, she lived in rural Coperhill, Tennessee so close to the Georgia border that she crossed the state line to attend kindergarten and first grade. When she was about six, she left Tennessee with her parents and lived the next 12 years in northern Kentucky and eastern Kansas. She moved to upstate Ithaca, New York to attend college at Cornell University, where she earned a bachelor's degree in 2000 and a master's degree in plant pathology in 2002. Two years later, she earned a master's degree in science writing from MIT. After school, she moved to Wyoming and worked as a reporter for three years in Cheyenne. She now lives, cooks (a lot!) and works as a science writer in Boulder, Colorado.

Ashley Frazer

Ashley Frazer, great-niece—Ashley Frazer is the daughter of Bohn and Linda Frazer, born Feburary 10, 1984. She attended the University of Kansas, where she played Division I softball and received a degree in electrical engineering. She is employed by the U.S. Government in the field of computer forensics. Ashley has many fond memories of dinner parties at Aunt Ethel's, which were notable for their generous dessert portions, wildly exaggerated (but expertly told) stories and doting hostess. Today they have inspired her own love of cooking and entertaining.

Bart, Sharie, Tucker and Regan Frazer

Robert B. "Bart" Frazer, great-nephew—Bart Frazer is the son of Bill and Sherry Frazer. He is married to Sharie Belt Frazer, daughter of Raymond and Sharon Belt. They have two children, Robert Tucker Frazer, 16, and a daughter, Regan Denise Frazer, 12. They reside in Marion, Kentucky where Bart is a practicing lawyer and Sharie is a retired school teacher.

Tom and Sara Ann Frazer and Maddye Mink

Sarah Ann Frazer Taylor, great-niece—Sarah Ann is the daughter of Bill and Sherry Frazer. She was born October 25, 1968. She and her husband Tom married in Louisville March 2010. They are both paramedics. Sarah's daughter Maddye, also the daughter of Jim Mink, was born January 26, 1999. She loves animals and music and wants to become a veterinarian. She is very active with the Mary Hall Ruddiman Canine Shelter in Marion.

Erica Guess

Erica Guess, great-niece—After graduating from Murray State University, Erica moved to San Francisco, California and took a job as a nanny for six-week-old twins. She is now working with her fifth set of twins and is considered a Newborn Twin Specialist. In addition, she is independently contracted as an Event Volunteer Coordinator for Compassion International, a Christian child sponsorship organization that has over 1 million children in 27 developing countries. When she's not working, she spends her time in servant and leadership positions at her church called Reality SF.

Katie, Kory, Crider and Finley Cunningham

Katie Stout Cunningham, great-niece—Kory and Katie Cunningham were married November 26, 2005. They have two children, Crider Cunningham, who was born on December 30, 2008, and Finley Cunningham, born Novemeber 23, 2010. Kory is the son of Rick and Celisa Cunningham of Dexter, Kentucky. He graduated from Murray State University in 2007 with a degree in organizational communications. Kory is a youth pastor at Hardin Baptist Church in Hardin, Kentucky, while pursuing a master of divinity degree from the Southern Baptist Theological Seminary in Louisville, Kentucky. Katie is the daughter of Alan and Doris Stout of Marion, Kentucky. She graduated from Murray State University in 2007 with a degree in Spanish. She currently stays at home raising the couple's children.

Logan Stout (center) with Doris and Alan Stout

Logan Stout, great-nephew—Logan is the son of Alan and Doris Stout. He graduated from Murray State University in May 2011 with a degree in Organizational Communication. He is attending Southern Baptist Theological Seminary in Louisville, Kentucky, seeking a Master of Divinity in Great Commission Ministries. Logan does sports broadcasting on the side.

Christmas 2010 at the Tucker residence (seated from left) Ethel Tucker, Alan Stout holding Finley Cunningham, Doris Stout holding Crider Cunningham; (standing) Logan Stout, Erica Guess and Katie and Kory Cunningham.

Jody, Jake and Annie Selph

Jacob Selph great-nephew—Jake Selph was born in Sarasota, Florida on November 8, 1975. He moved to Marion, Kentucky in 1992 and graduated from Crittenden County High School in 1994. He graduated from the University of Louisville with a Master of Civil Engineering in 2005. In 2006, he married Jody Beth Summers, and had a daughter, Anna Marie Selph, born July 1, 2009. Jake is the owner of Four Rivers Engineering and Surveying located in Eddyville, Kentucky.

Chapter 2

Party Fare, Snacks, Sandwiches & Beverages

Ham Spinach Balls

1 cup ground ham
1 cup frozen chopped spinach, cooked according to directions
(drain well)
2 tablespoons horseradish/mustard
3 ounces cream cheese
Approximately ½ to ¾ cup of bread crumbs
Seasonings: Minced garlic, lemon pepper, or essence seasonings

Mix all together and chill. Make into small balls and bake at 350° for 10 minutes. Cool to touch and roll in chopped parsley. May be made ahead of time.

Chicken Salad Tarts

Yields 5 dozen appetizers

2¼ cups all-purpose flour
½ teaspoon salt
½ cup shortening
¼ cup butter or margarine
½ to ⅔ cup milk
4 cups finely chopped cooked chicken
2 stalks celery, finely chopped
½ cup slivered almonds, toasted
⅔ cup of mayonnaise
2 tablespoons commercial steak sauce
½ teaspoon curry powder
¼ teaspoon garlic salt
Pimiento strips

Combine flour and salt; cut in shortening and butter with pastry blender until mixture resembles coarse meal. Sprinkle milk (1 tablespoon at a time) evenly over surface; stir with a fork just until dry ingredients are moistened. Shape dough into about 60 (¾-inch) balls. Place in ungreased 1¾ inch muffin pans, and shape each ball into a shell. Bake at 400° for 10-12 minutes. Cool.

Combine next 8 ingredients; mix well. Cover and chill at least 1 hour; spoon into tart shells. Garnish with pimiento strips.

Cocktail Sausage

Yields 4-6 servings

1 pound miniature smoked sausage links
1 cup barbeque sauce
¼ cup orange marmalade

In a large skillet, combine sausage and barbecue sauce; stir over medium heat until heated through. Gradually stir in marmalade. Serve warm.

Mini Taco Cups

Yields 24 cups

½ pound mild pork sausage
½ pound ground chuck
1 (8 ounce) jar taco sauce
½ cup (2 ounces) shredded Monterey Jack cheese
1 (4.5 ounce) can chopped green chiles
1 (16 ounce) package won ton wrappers

Toppings:
Sour cream
Shredded cheese
Salsa
Chopped lettuce

Crumble sausage and ground beef into a microwave-safe container. Microwave at high 1 minute, and stir. Microwave at high 4 to 4½ minutes, stirring every 60 seconds or until meat is done and no longer pink. Drain well on paper towels. Stir together sausage mixture, taco sauce, ½ cup shredded cheese, and green chiles. Set aside.

Press won ton wrappers into 24 lightly greased mini muffin cups. Reserve remaining wrappers for another use.

Bake at 350° for 8 minutes or until wrappers start to brown. Remove muffin pans to wire racks. Fill baked won ton cups evenly with sausage mixture. Return pans to oven, and bake 15 more minutes or until thoroughly heated and cheese melts. Serve with desired toppings.

Pizza Appetizers

2 pounds hamburger
1 pound sausage
2 pounds Velveeta cheese
1 tablespoon Italian seasoning
2 packages cocktail rye bread

Brown hamburger and sausage. Drain well. Add Italian seasoning and melted cheese. Mix and cover the rye bread. Bake at 350° until hot, about 10-15 minutes. Freezes well.

Ranch Chicken Nuggets

Yields 2½ dozen nuggets

1 cup panko (Japanese bread crumbs)
2 tablespoons dry ranch seasoning mix
½ teaspoon salt
1 pound boneless skinless chicken breasts, cut into 1-inch cubes
¾ cup all-purpose flour
1 large egg, lightly beaten
Vegetable oil for frying
Prepared barbeque sauce

In a small bowl, combine panko, seasoning mix, and salt; set aside.

Dredge chicken cubes in flour. Dip in beaten egg, then coat in panko mixture.

Pour oil to a depth of 2 inches in a large Dutch oven. Heat to 360°. Fry chicken nuggets, in batches, for 5-6 minutes, or until done. Serve with barbeque sauce.

Country Ham Cups

Yields 24 servings

2 cups ground cooked ham
2 cups shredded sharp cheddar cheese
½ cup mayonnaise
24 slices white bread

Combine the ham, cheese, and mayonnaise in a bowl and mix well, adding additional mayonnaise if needed. Cut a circle from each slice of bread using a biscuit cutter. Place between 2 sheets of waxed paper and flatten with rolling pin. Press into muffin cups sprayed with nonstick cooking spray. Bake at 375° for 10 minutes or until light brown. Reduce the oven temperature to 325°. Fill each cup with the ham mixture. Bake for 15 minutes or until the cheese is melted. Serve hot.

Spicy Party Mix

Yields 8 cups

6 tablespoons butter or oleo
1 (1 ounce) envelope cheese Italian salad dressing mix
1 teaspoon Worcestershire sauce
⅛ teaspoon garlic powder
⅛ teaspoon hot sauce
4 cups bite-size crispy corn or wheat square cereal
3 cups pretzel sticks
1 cup mixed salted nuts

Place butter in a large glass mixing bowl; microwave at high for 45 seconds to 1 minute or until butter melts. Stir in next 4 ingredients.

Add cereal, pretzel sticks, and nuts to butter mixture; toss gently. Microwave at medium for 3 to 5 minutes or until thoroughly heated, stirring after 2 minutes. Let cool, and store in an airtight container.

Cheese Straws

Yields about 6 dozen

1½ cups all-purpose flour
1 teaspoon baking powder
1 teaspoon salt
⅛ teaspoon sugar
1 teaspoon red pepper
⅓ cup butter or margarine
1 cup shredded sharp cheddar cheese
¼ cup cold water

Combine first 5 ingredients, mixing well. Melt butter and let cool. Pour over cheese, and toss gently. Add to dry ingredients, and cut in until mixture resembles coarse meal. Sprinkle water evenly over flour mixture; stir with a fork until all ingredients are moistened. Shape into a ball.

Roll dough to ⅛-inch thickness on a lightly floured surface, and cut into 3½-inch strips.

Place strips on ungreased cookie sheets. Bake at 325° for 10-12 minutes or until crisp. Place on wire racks to cool.

Benedictine Sandwich Spread

1 large cucumber
1 (8 ounce) package cream cheese, softened
1 small onion, minced
¼ teaspoon salt
1 tablespoon mayonnaise
2-3 drops green food coloring

Pare, grate, and drain cucumber. Combine cucumber with other ingredients. Serve on crackers, or make small sandwiches with white bread.

Barbequed Frankfurters

Yields 6 servings

12 frankfurters, scored diagonally
1 small onion, sliced
1 tablespoon butter or margarine
½ cup ketchup
½ cup water
2 tablespoons sugar
¼ cup vinegar
1 tablespoon plus 1 teaspoon Worcestershire sauce
1 teaspoon celery salt
1 teaspoon dry mustard
½ teaspoon paprika
½ teaspoon hot sauce

Place frankfurters in a 12x8x2-inch baking dish; set aside.

Sauté onion in butter in a medium saucepan until tender. Remove from heat; stir in remaining ingredients. Pour over frankfurters. Bake, uncovered, at 325° for 25 minutes.

Spiced Cider Punch

Yields 6 quarts

2 quarts apple cider
1 (3-inch) sticks of cinnamon
12 whole cloves
2 cups pineapple juice, chilled
1½ quarts orange juice, chilled
2 cups lemon juice, chilled
1½ quarts ginger ale, chilled

Combine cider, cinnamon, and cloves in a Dutch oven; bring to a boil. Cover, reduce heat, and simmer 15 minutes. Strain cider to remove cinnamon and cloves; chill. Combine cider and juice.

Just before serving, combine juice mixture and ginger ale in a punch bowl.

Fruit Slush Punch

Yields 2½ gallons (2½ quarts per bag of mixture)
2½ quarts water
3 (6 ounce) cans frozen lemonade concentrate, thawed and undiluted
2 (46 ounce) cans unsweetened pineapple juice
2 (0.14 ounce) envelopes cherry or lemon-lime flavored
unsweetened drink mix
8 (10 ounce) bottles ginger ale

Combine all ingredients except ginger ale; stir until drink mix dissolves. Divide mixture evenly into 4 gallon-size, heavy-duty, zip-top plastic bags; freeze. Remove each bag from freezer 1 hour before serving. Place in a punch bowl, and break into chunks; add 2 bottles ginger ale to each bag of mixture. Stir until slushy.

Citrus Iced Tea

Yields 5 cups

3 cups water
2 whole cloves
1 family-sized tea bag
1½ cups pineapple juice
½ cup orange juice
2 to 4 tablespoons fresh lemon juice
⅔ cup of sugar
Garnishes: fresh mint sprigs, orange juice

Bring 3 cups of water and cloves to a boil over medium heat; reduce heat, and simmer 10 minutes. Remove from heat, and add tea bag; steep 10 minutes.

Discard tea bag and cloves. Add fruit juices and sugar, stirring until sugar dissolves. Chill and serve over crushed ice. Garnish if desired.

Hot Cranberry Cider

Yields 32 servings

3 quarts apple cider
1 quart cranberry juice cocktail
¼ cup sugar
3 oranges
16 whole cloves
6 cinnamon sticks
1 teaspoon allspice

Combine cider, cranberry juice, and sugar. Pierce oranges. Place oranges and spices in a bag or in a coffee basket if using a percolator. Serve hot, cold, or at room temperature.

Boiled Custard

2 cups of sugar
5 tablespoons cornstarch
½ gallon milk
4 egg yolks
1 teaspoon vanilla

In a 2½ quart casserole, mix sugar and cornstarch well. Gradually stir in milk. Microwave on high for 15 minutes. Stir well. Microwave high 8-10 minutes until slightly thickened. Beat egg yolks and gradually stir in some of cooked mixture. Return egg mixture to casserole, mixing well. Microwave on medium 2-4 minutes. Stir in vanilla. Cool.

Chapter 3

Breads, Rolls, Muffins & Coffee Cakes

My Roll Recipe

Over the years I have tried several roll recipes, but this is the one that is consistently the best.

1 package of yeast in ¼ cup of warm yeast and 1 teaspoon of sugar
1½ cups scalded milk
½ cup Crisco shortening
2 eggs, well beaten
½ cup sugar
1½ teaspoons salt
4½ cups unbleached flour

Add sugar, shortening, and salt to scalded milk in large mixing bowl. Cool and add well beaten eggs, yeast, and flour. Mix well and cover bowl and allow to rise about 1 hour until doubled. Turn out onto floured board and knead lightly. Divide dough and roll each to ½-inch thickness, cut with desired sized cutter and place in well-greased pan. Let rise in warm place, covered, for 1 to 1½ hours until doubled in size. Bake in 375° oven until done, about 18 minutes. Brush with melted butter.

Whole Wheat Dinner Rolls

Yields 4 dozen

2 packages (¼ ounces each) active dry yeast
2¼ cups warm water (110°-115°)
¼ cup shortening
2 eggs
½ cup plus 1 tablespoon sugar
2 teaspoons salt
3 cups whole wheat flour
3½-4 cups of all-purpose flour
¼ cup butter or margarine, melted

In a large mixing bowl, dissolve yeast in warm water; let stand for 5 minutes. Add the shortening, eggs, sugar, salt, and whole wheat flour; beat until smooth. Add enough all-purpose flour to form a soft dough. Turn onto a floured surface; knead until smooth and elastic, about 6-8 minutes. Place in a greased bowl, turning once to grease top. Cover and let rise in a warm place until doubled, about 1 hour. Punch dough down. Divide into four portions; shape each into 12 balls. Place 1 inch apart on greased baking sheets. Cover and let rise until doubled, about 25 minutes. Bake at 375° for 11-15 minutes or until browned. Brush with butter.

Best Rolls

Yields about 3 dozen rolls

1 cup shortening
1 scant cup sugar
1½ cups boiling water
1½ teaspoons salt
½ cup warm water
2 packages yeast
6 cups unsifted flour
2 eggs, beaten

Measure shortening and sugar into bowl. Pour boiling water on top and add salt. Blend and set aside. Sprinkle yeast into ½ cup warm water.

Mix 2 cups flour with shortening mixture. Add beaten eggs and blend. Add 2 cups flour and mix well. Add yeast mixture and blend. Add last 2 cups flour and mix well. Cover and refrigerate in a large bowl for 4 hours. Knead and shape into shape into rolls 2 to 3 hours before serving. Put in lightly greased pan, and let rise until doubled in size. Bake at 375° to 400° for 12-15 minutes.

Hurry-Up Homemade Crescent Rolls

1 (¼ ounce) envelope active dry yeast
¾ cup warm water (105°-115°)
3-3½ cups all-purpose baking mix
2 tablespoons sugar
All-purpose flour

Combine yeast and warm water in a 1-cup measuring cup; let stand 5 minutes. Combine 3 cups baking mix and sugar in a large bowl; gradually stir in yeast mixture. Turn dough out onto a floured surface, and knead, adding additional baking mix (up to ½ cup) as needed, until dough is smooth and elastic (about 10 minutes). Rolling dough into a 12-inch circle; cut circle into 12 wedges. Roll up wedges, starting at wide end, to form a crescent shape; place, point sides down, on a lightly greased baking sheet. Cover and let rise in a warm place, free from drafts, 1 hour or until doubled in bulk. Preheat oven to 425°. Bake 10 to 12 minutes or until golden.

Daisy Biscuits

Yields 28 biscuits

1 (3 ounce) package cream cheese
¼ cup butter or margarine
2½ cups self-rising flour
¾ cup milk
2½ tablespoons orange marmalade
2½ tablespoons raspberry jam

Cut cream cheese and butter into flour with a pastry blender until mixture resembles coarse meal. Add milk, stirring until dry ingredients are moistened. Turn dough out onto a floured surface, and knead 3 or 4 times.

Roll dough to ½-inch thickness; cut with a 2-inch biscuit cutter. Place on an ungreased baking sheet. Make 6 slits, through dough around edges of each biscuit to ¼ inch from center. Press thumb in center of each biscuit, leaving an indentation. Spoon ½ teaspoon marmalade or jam into each biscuit indentation. Bake at 450° for 10-12 minutes or until golden brown.

Cheese Biscuits

Yields 1½ dozen

2 cups all-purpose flour
3 teaspoons baking powder
¾ teaspoon salt
¼ cup shortening
¾ cup milk
¼ to ½ cup sharp cheddar cheese, shredded

Preheat oven to 450°. Sift flour and measure. Add baking powder and salt and sift together or stir together to mix. Stir shredded cheese into flour mixture. Cut shortening into dry mixture with a pastry blender or two table knives until it is as fine as coarse crumbs. Add milk and stir in with a fork.

Turn dough out on a lightly floured board or pastry cloth and knead just until smooth. Roll dough out about ½-inch thick and cut with a floured cutter. Place biscuits on a lightly greased baking sheet and bake 10-12 minutes.

Dorothy's Biscuits

2 cups flour
6 level teaspoons baking powder
½ teaspoon salt
3 heaping tablespoons Crisco
Buttermilk
Melted butter

Sift flour, salt, and baking powder into a mixing bowl. Work the Crisco into flour mixture with hand or fork.

Pour buttermilk and stir so it looks like soft dough. Turn onto well floured board and work very lightly. Roll or pat out and cut with floured cutter. Place on greased baking sheet and brush with melted butter. Bake in hot 450° oven for 10-12 minutes or until brown.

Dorothy Frazer was my sister-in-law and she made the best biscuits I ever did eat. I watched her and wrote the above recipe, yet I can still not make them taste as good or be as light as hers. I think I work the dough too much. She worked the shortening with her hands and I haven't learned to do it.

Old-Fashion Cinnamon Rolls

Yields 24 rolls

4¾ to 5¼ cups all-purpose flour
1 package active dry yeast
1 cup milk
⅓ cup butter
⅓ cup granulated sugar
3 eggs
3 tablespoons butter, melted
⅔ cup sugar
2 teaspoons ground cinnamon
Creamy Glaze

In a large bowl combine 2¼ cups flour and yeast. In a saucepan, heat and stir milk, ⅓ cup granulated sugar, and ½ teaspoon salt just until warm (120°-130°) and butter almost melts. Add to flour mixture; add eggs. Beat on low speed for 30 seconds, scraping bowl. Beat on high speed for 3 minutes. Stir in as much of remaining flour as you can.

On a lightly floured surface knead in enough of the remaining flour to make moderately soft dough that is smooth and elastic (3-5 minutes total). Shape into a ball. Place in greased bowl, turning once. Cover, let rise in warm place until doubled in size (1 hour).

Punch down dough. Turn out onto lightly floured surface; divide in half. Cover and let rest 10 minutes. Lightly grease two 9x1½ inch round baking pans. Roll each half of the dough into a 12x8 rectangle. Brush with melted butter. Combine the ⅔ cup sugar and the cinnamon; sprinkle over rectangles. Starting from the long side, roll up each rectangle into a spiral. Seal seams. Cut each spiral into 12 slices. Place slices, cut sides down, in prepared pans.

Cover dough loosely with plastic wrap, leaving room for rolls to rise. Chill for at least 2 hours or up to 24 hours. Uncover; let stand at room temperature for 30 minutes.

Preheat oven to 375°. Break surface bubbles with a greased toothpick. Bake for 20 to 25 minutes or until light brown. If necessary to prevent over-browning, cover rolls loosely with foil for the last 5 to 10 minutes of baking. Remove from oven. Cool for 1 minute. Carefully invert rolls onto wire rack. Cool slightly. Invert again onto a serving platter. Drizzle with Creamy Glaze. Serve warm.

Creamy Glaze

1¼ cups sifted powdered sugar
1 teaspoon light-colored corn syrup
½ teaspoon vanilla
1 to 2 tablespoons half and half or light cream

Mix 1 ¼ cups sifted powdered sugar, 1 teaspoon light-colored corn syrup, and ½ teaspoon vanilla. Stir in enough half-and-half or light cream (1 to 2 tablespoons) to make of drizzling consistency.

Best-Ever Blueberry Muffins

1½ cups all-purpose flour
1 tablespoon baking powder
½ teaspoon salt
¼ cup sugar
4 tablespoons (½ stick) unsalted butter, melted and cooled
1 large egg, beaten
¾ cup plus 2 tablespoons milk
1 cup blueberries

Preheat oven to 400°. Line a muffin pan with 10 paper muffin cups or spray with nonstick cooking spray. Fill empty cups halfway with water.

Sift the flour, baking powder and salt into a large bowl. Stir in the sugar. In a separate bowl, whisk together the melted butter, egg and milk. Pour in the wet ingredients and whisk until just blended (mixture should be slightly lumpy).

Add blueberries to bowl and stir them in just enough to combine.

Divide the batter evenly among the prepared muffin cups. Bake the muffins until golden, 18-24 minutes. Remove the muffins from the pan and transfer to a wire rack to cool. Muffins are best served warm.

Cream Cheese Banana Nut Bread

Makes 2 loaves

¾ cup butter, softened
1 (8 ounce) package cream cheese, softened
2 cups sugar
2 large eggs
3 cups all-purpose flour
½ teaspoon baking powder
½ teaspoon baking soda
½ teaspoon salt
½ cup mashed bananas (1¼ pounds unpeeled bananas, about 4 medium)
1 cup chopped pecans, toasted
½ teaspoon vanilla extract

Beat butter and cream cheese at medium speed with an electric mixer until creamy. Gradually add sugar, beating until light and fluffy. Add eggs, 1 at a time, beating just until blended after each addition.

Combine flour and next 3 ingredients; gradually add to butter mixture, beating at low speed just until blended. Stir in bananas, pecans, and vanilla. Spoon batter into 2 greased and floured 8 x 4 inch loaf pans.

Bake at 350° for 1 hour or until a long wooden pick inserted in center comes out clean and sides pull away from pan, shielding with aluminum foil last 15 minutes to prevent browning, if necessary. Cool bread in pans on wire racks 10 minutes. Remove from pans and cool 30 minutes on wire racks before slicing.

Sweet Potato Biscuits

Yields about 17 (2-inch) biscuits
1 egg, slightly beaten
1 cup cooked, mashed sweet potatoes
¼ to ½ cup sugar
2 tablespoons butter or margarine, softened
3 tablespoons shortening
About 2 cups self-rising flour

Combine egg, sweet potatoes, sugar, butter, and shortening in a mixing bowl; mix well. Stir in enough flour to make soft dough. (Dough will be softer than regular biscuit dough.)

Turn out on a floured surface; knead lightly a few times. Roll to ¼-inch thickness; cut with a 2-inch biscuit cutter. Place on an ungreased baking sheet and bake at 350° about 15 minutes.

Note: Use ¼ cup sugar if potatoes are naturally sweet and juicy.

Date Coffee Cake

Yields 8-10 servings

⅓ cup mashed ripe banana (mash ripe banana with a fork)
½ cup butter, softened
3 large eggs
1 teaspoon vanilla extract
1¼ cups water
3 cups unbleached white flour
½ teaspoon salt
1 teaspoon baking soda
2 teaspoons baking powder
1½ cups chopped dates

Topping:
⅓ cup chopped dates
⅓ cup chopped walnuts
⅓ cup flaked coconut

Beat together mashed banana and butter until creamy. Add eggs, vanilla extract, and water; beat. Measure in flour, baking soda, and baking powder, beat well. Stir in 1½ cups chopped dates. Spoon batter into an oiled and floured 9x13-inch baking pan. Spread batter evenly in pan.

Combine topping ingredients and sprinkle over batter. Bake at 350° for 20-25 minutes or until a knife inserted comes out clean. Cool on wire rack.

Apple Pull-Apart Bread

Yields 1 loaf

1 package (¼ ounce) active dry yeast
1 cup warm milk (110° to 115°)
½ cup butter or margarine, melted, divided
1 egg
⅔ cup plus 2 tablespoons sugar, divided
1 teaspoon salt
3 to 3½ cups all-purpose flour
1 medium tart apple, peeled and chopped
½ cup finely chopped pecans
½ teaspoon ground cinnamon

Icing:
1 cup confectioners' sugar
3 to 4½ teaspoons hot water
½ teaspoon vanilla extract

In a mixing bowl, dissolve yeast in milk. Add 2 tablespoons butter, egg, 2 tablespoons sugar, salt and 3 cups flour; beat until smooth. Add enough remaining flour to form a stiff dough. Turn onto a floured surface; knead until smooth and elastic, 6-8 minutes. Place in a greased bowl, turning once to grease top. Cover and let rise in a warm place until doubled, about 1 hour. Combine apple, pecans, cinnamon, and remaining sugar, set aside. Punch dough down; divide in half. Cut each half into 16 pieces. On a lightly floured surface, pat or roll out each piece into 2½-inch circle. Place 1 teaspoon apple mixture in center or circle; pinch edges together and seal, forming a ball. Dip in remaining butter. In a greased 10-inch tube pan, place 16 balls, seam side down; sprinkle with ¼ cup apple mixture. Layer remaining balls; sprinkle with remaining apple mixture. Cover and let rise until nearly doubled, about 45 minutes. Bake at 350° for 35-40 minutes or until golden brown. Cool for 10 minutes; remove from pan to a wire rack. Combine icing ingredients; drizzle over bread.

Sour Cream Coffee Cake

Yields 10 servings

3 cups all-purpose flour
1½ teaspoons baking powder
1½ teaspoons baking soda
¼ teaspoon salt
1½ cups (3 sticks) butter, room temperature
1½ cups sugar
3 eggs
1½ teaspoons vanilla
1½ cups sour cream
¾ cup firmly packed brown sugar
¾ cup chopped walnuts
1½ teaspoons cinnamon
2 tablespoons vanilla mixed with 2 tablespoons water
Powdered sugar (garnish)

Preheat oven to 375°. Butter 10-inch tube pan. Sift together first 4 ingredients; set aside. Combine butter and sugar in large bowl and beat until fluffy. Add eggs one at a time, beating well after each addition. Blend in sour cream and vanilla. Gradually add sifted dry ingredients and beat well.

Combine brown sugar, walnuts, and cinnamon in small bowl. Turn ⅓ of batter into prepared pan and sprinkle with half of nut mixture. Repeat. Add remaining batter and spoon diluted vanilla over top. Bake 60 to 70 minutes. Cool 10 minutes before removing from pan (texture will be moist). Dust generously with powdered sugar.

Sour Cream Coffee Cake Muffins

1 cup butter, softened
2 cups sugar
2 large eggs
1 cup sour cream
½ teaspoon vanilla extract
2 cups all-purpose flour
1 teaspoon baking powder
¼ teaspoon salt
⅛ teaspoon baking soda
24 paper baking cups
1 cup pecans, finely chopped
¼ cup sugar
1½ teaspoons ground cinnamon

Preheat oven 350°. Beat butter at medium speed with an electric mixer 2 minutes or until creamy. Gradually add 2 cups sugar, beating 2 to 3 minutes. Add eggs, 1 at a time, beating until blended after each addition. Add sour cream and vanilla, beating until blended.

Whisk together flour and next 3 ingredients; gradually stir into butter mixture. (Batter will be thick)

Place baking cups in muffin pans. Spoon batter into cups, filling ⅔ full.

Stir together pecans, ¼ cup sugar, and cinnamon. Sprinkle pecan mixture over batter.

Bake 350° for 20-25 minutes or until a wooden pick inserted in center comes out clean. Remove from pans, and cool completely on wire racks (about 13-15 minutes).

Chapter 4

Pasta, Eggs & Cheese

Spanish Scrambled Eggs

Yields 6 servings

½ pound bacon
1 dozen eggs, beaten
1 (4 ounce) can chopped green chiles, drained
1 (4 ounce) jar diced pimiento, drained
¼ cup butter or margarine
1 bunch green onions, finely chopped
1 large tomato, chopped
1 (4½ ounce) jar sliced mushrooms, drained
tomato roses

Cook bacon in a large skillet until crisp. Remove bacon; crumble and set aside. Discard drippings.

Combine eggs, chiles, and pimiento; set aside. Melt butter in skillet. Add onions, tomato, and mushrooms; sauté until tender. Add egg mixture; cook over medium heat, stirring often, until eggs are firm but still moist. Spoon onto serving platter; garnish with crumbled bacon and tomato roses.

Polenta Parmesan

4 cups water
1 teaspoon salt
1¼ cups yellow cornmeal
Butter
½ to 1 cup freshly grated Parmesan cheese

Bring water to a boil and add salt. Lower heat and stir in the cornmeal, a little at a time, stirring constantly to prevent lumping and sticking. (A whisk is good for this if you have one.) Cook 15 minutes, or until polenta is very thick. Pour into a greased bread pan (8 by 4½ inches) and refrigerate until cool. Run a knife around the edge of the pan and remove the loaf.

Cut the polenta into ½-inch-thick slices and place overlapping in a large, flat casserole. Dot between the slices with butter, then sprinkle the slices with freshly grated Parmesan cheese. (The polenta can be assembled ahead of time to this point and refrigerated.)

Bake in a 350° oven until cheese is melted and edges are brown, about 25 minutes.

Biscuit Bites

1 tube (12 ounces) refrigerated buttermilk biscuits
2 tablespoons grated Parmesan cheese
1 teaspoon onion powder

Cut each biscuit into thirds; place on a greased baking sheet. Combine Parmesan cheese and onion powder; sprinkle over biscuits. Bake at 400° for 7-8 minutes or until golden brown.

Creole Hominy

Yields 4 servings

4 slices of bacon
1 medium onion, chopped medium-fine
1 medium green pepper, seeded and chopped medium-fine
16-ounce can stewed tomatoes
16-ounce can whole yellow hominy, drained
½ to 1 tablespoon sugar if desired

Salt and pepper to taste in a 10-inch skillet over a low heat cook the bacon until crisp; remove and drain on brown paper; crumble. Pour off all but 2 tablespoons of bacon fat from the skillet; add onion and green pepper; cook gently, stirring often, until wilted. Add tomatoes, hominy, sugar, salt and pepper; simmer until hot and liquid has been absorbed. Sprinkle with the bacon. Serve hot.

Garlic Grits

1 cup of grits
1 package garlic cheese
1 stick butter
2 eggs
Milk
½ teaspoon paprika
1 cup of shredded cheese

Heat oven to 300°. Cook as directed on the package 1 cup of grits (should be "soupy"). Mix 1 package of garlic cheese, 1 stick of butter, and then break the 2 eggs into a measuring cup (fill remainder of cup with milk up to 1 cup). Bake for 45 minutes. Remove and add shredded cheese and paprika to top and place back in oven for 10 more minutes.

Grits

1 cup grits
1 quart sweet milk
½ cup of butter cut in pieces
1 cup grated cheese
⅓ cup Parmesan cheese

Cook 1 cup of grits with 1 one quart of sweet milk. Use a good bit to butter dish. Combine and add other ingredients. Cook at 400° degrees for 30-35 minutes.

Savory Ham And Swiss Breakfast Pie

1⅔ cups water
1 cup whipping cream
2 garlic cloves, pressed
2 tablespoons butter
1 teaspoon of salt
¼ teaspoon pepper
⅔ cup uncooked quick-cooking grits
1¼ cups (5 ounces) shredded Swiss cheese, divided
8 large eggs, divided
½ pound cooked ham, diced
4 green onions, chopped
½ cup milk
Chives for garnish

Bring first 6 ingredients to a boil in a medium saucepan; gradually whisk in grits. Cover, reduce heat, and simmer, whisking occasionally, 5 to 7 minutes. Add ½ cup cheese, stirring until cheese melts. Remove from heat, and let stand 10 minutes. Lightly beat 2 eggs, and stir into grits mixture; pour into a lightly greased 10-inch-deep pie plate.

Bake at 350° for 20 minutes; remove from oven. Increase oven temperature to 400°. Sauté ham and onions in a nonstick skillet over medium-high heat 5 minutes or until onion is tender. Layer ham mixture evenly over grits crust. Whisk together milk and remaining 6 eggs; pour over ham mixture. Sprinkle remaining ¾ cup of cheese evenly over egg mixture. Bake at 400° for 35 minutes. Let stand 10 minutes, and cut into wedges. Garnish if desired.

Egg-Mushroom Casserole

8 eggs, beaten
1 cup milk
¼ teaspoon salt
⅛ teaspoon pepper
2 cups cooked rice
1 (4½ ounce) jar sliced mushrooms, drained
Cheese Sauce (recipe follows)

Combine first 4 ingredients; mix will. Stir in rice and mushrooms; pour into a buttered 12x8x2-inch baking dish. Bake at 350° for 30 to 35 minutes or until set. Cut into squares, and serve immediately with cheese sauce.

Cheese Sauce

Yields about 1½ cups

2 tablespoons butter or margarine
2 tablespoons all-purpose flour
1⅓ cups of milk
1 cup (4 ounces) shredded cheddar cheese
½ teaspoon salt
⅛ teaspoon pepper
Pinch of sugar

Melt butter in a heavy saucepan over low heat; add flour, and stir until smooth. Cook 1 minute, stirring constantly. Gradually add milk; cook over medium heat, stirring constantly, until thickened and bubbly. Add cheese, salt, and pepper, stirring until cheese melts.

Cheese Custard

12 saltine crackers
2 cups milk
1 cup grated cheese
3 eggs
1 stick butter
Salt
Pepper

Crumble crackers in greased casserole dish. Cover with cheese. Mix eggs, butter, and milk; pour over crackers and cheese. Let stand 30 minutes. Bake at 400° until set. Serve at once.

Gourmet Wild Rice

Yields 6 servings

⅓ cup currants
2 tablespoons brandy
⅔ cup wild rice
2 cups ready-to-serve chicken broth
2 tablespoons olive oil
⅓ cup pine nuts, toasted

Combine currants and brandy, and set aside.

Wash wild rice in 3 changes of hot water; drain. Combine rice and chicken broth in a medium saucepan; bring to a boil. Cover, reduce heat, and simmer 45 minutes or until rice is tender and liquid is absorbed. Stir in currant mixture, olive oil, and pine nuts.

Cheese Soufflé

½ cup butter
1 cup milk
4 eggs
Dash of paprika
¼ cup flour
1 cup grated sharp cheese
1 teaspoon salt
¼ teaspoon dry mustard

Make a thick sauce with butter, flour, and milk. Remove from heat. Add cheese and seasoning. Stir until cheese is melted. Add well-beaten egg yolks. Fold in stiffly beaten egg whites. Pour into buttered baking dish and place dish in pan of hot water and bake at 350° for 1 hour. Never fails!

Taco Quiche

Yields 8 servings

2 pounds ground beef
2 envelopes taco seasoning
4 eggs
¾ cup milk
1¼ cups biscuit/baking mix
Dash of pepper
½ cup sour cream
2 to 3 cups chopped lettuce
¾ cup chopped tomato
¾ cup chopped green pepper
¼ cup chopped green onions
2 cups (8 ounces) shredded cheddar cheese

In a skillet, brown beef; drain. Add taco seasoning and prepare according to the package directions. Spoon meat into a greased 13x9-inch baking dish. In a bowl, beat eggs and milk. Add biscuit mix and pepper; mix well. Pour over meat. Bake, uncovered, at 400° for 20-25 minutes or until golden brown. Cool for 5-10 minutes. Spread sour cream over the top; sprinkle with lettuce, tomato, green pepper, onions and cheese. Serve immediately.

Ham And Cheese Layered Casserole

Yields 6 servings

12 (¾ inch-thick) Italian bread slices
1 cup chopped cooked ham
2 cups shredded mozzarella cheese, divided
3 large eggs
2 cups of milk
½ teaspoon a garlic powder
¼ teaspoon onion powder
¼ teaspoon pepper

Place 6 bread slices in a lightly greased 11x7-inch baking dish. Sprinkle with ham and 1 cup of cheese. Top with remaining bread slices. Stir together eggs and next 4 ingredients; pour over bread. Bake at 350° for 40 minutes. Sprinkle with remaining 1 cup of cheese; bake 5 more minutes. Let stand 5 minutes before serving.

Texas Grits Soufflé

Serves 12-14

6 cups very lightly salted water
1½ cup of grits
1 pound grated cheddar cheese
1½ sticks of butter
3 whole eggs, beaten
¼ teaspoon of salt, white pepper, and garlic powder
¼ teaspoon of Tabasco

Boil water and add grits, cooking and stirring until mixture is thick. Remove from heat and add grated cheddar cheese and butter. Stir until smooth. Add eggs, salt, pepper, and garlic powder, and Tabasco. Mix well and pour into an 11x14-inch oiled baking dish. Bake 1 hour in preheated 250° oven.

Ham and Mushroom Quiche

Yields two 9-inch quiches
Pastry for two 9-inch quiche dishes or pie plates
1 bunch green onions, chopped
2 tablespoons melted butter or margarine
2 cups shredded Swiss cheese
6 slices of bacon, cooked and crumbled
1 (8 ounce) can sliced mushrooms, drained
2 cups coarsely shredded ham
8 eggs, beaten
1½ cups evaporated milk
1 clove garlic, crushed
½ teaspoon salt
½ teaspoon dry mustard
Dash of ground nutmeg
Dash of white pepper

Line two 9-inch quiche dishes or pie plates with pastry; trim excess pastry from edges. Fold edges under and flute. Prick bottom and sides of pastry with a fork. Bake at 425° for 6 to 8 minutes. Let cool on wire rack.

Sauté onion in butter until tender. Combine onion, cheese, bacon, mushrooms, and ham; toss gently. Spoon half of mixture into each pastry shell.

Combine remaining ingredients; beat well. Pour half of egg mixture into each pastry shell. Bake at 350° for 30-40 minutes or until set.

Note: Unbaked quiche may be covered with aluminum foil and frozen. To serve, thaw overnight in refrigerator; bake at 350° for 40-50 minutes.

BLT Egg Bake

Yields 4 servings

¼ cup mayonnaise
5 slices of bread, toasted
4 slices processed American cheese
12 bacon strips, cooked and crumbled
4 eggs
1 medium tomato, halved and sliced
2 tablespoons butter or margarine
2 tablespoons all-purpose flour
¼ teaspoon salt
⅛ teaspoon pepper
1 cup of milk
½ cup shredded cheddar cheese
2 green onions, thinly sliced
Shredded lettuce

Spread mayonnaise on one side of each slice of toast and cut into small pieces. Arrange toast, mayonnaise side up, in a greased 8-inch square baking dish. Top with cheese slices and bacon. In a skillet, fry eggs over medium heat until completely set; place over bacon. Top with tomato slices; set aside.

In a saucepan melt butter. Stir in flour, salt and pepper until smooth. Gradually add milk. Bring to a boil; cook and stir for 2 minutes or until thickened. Pour over tomato. Sprinkle with cheddar cheese and onions. Bake uncovered, at 325° for 10 minutes. Cut into squares and serve with lettuce.

Ham-Rice-Tomato Bake

Yields 4 servings

2 cups cooked diced ham
1 cup cooked rice
½ cup chopped onion
¼ cup chopped green pepper
1 (4 ounce) can mushrooms, stems and pieces, drained
1 (16 ounce) can stewed tomatoes, chopped and *not* drained
¼ teaspoon salt
¼ teaspoon pepper
1 cup soft bread crumbs
¼ cup butter or margarine, melted

Heat oven to 350°. Combine first 8 ingredients; mix well. Spoon into a greased 2-quart casserole. Combine bread crumbs and butter; toss to mix well. Sprinkle on top of casserole. Bake uncovered for 30 minutes.

Main Dish Tart

Yields 6 main-dish servings
10-inch unbaked pie shell
½ pound bacon, cooked until crisp and crumbled
¼ pound Swiss cheese, coarsely grated
4 large eggs
1 pint light cream
½ teaspoon salt
½ of a 10-ounce package of frozen chopped spinach (cooked, drained, and lightly pressed out)

Preheat oven to 425°. Sprinkle pie shell with the bacon and cheese. Beat together the eggs, cream and salt just until blended; stir in spinach; pour over bacon and cheese. Bake in preheated oven for 15 minutes; continue baking at 300° until a knife inserted 1 inch from the edge comes out clean, about 30 minutes. Let stand about 10 minutes before cutting.

Country Grits and Sausage

Yields 8-10 servings
2 cups of water
½ teaspoon salt
½ cup uncooked quick grits
4 cups shredded extra-sharp cheddar cheese
4 eggs, beaten
1 cup milk
½ teaspoon dried whole thyme
⅛ teaspoon garlic salt
2 pounds mild bulk pork sausage, cooked, crumbled, and drained
Tomato roses
Parsley

Bring water and salt to a boil; stir in grits. Return to a boil; reduce heat. Cook 4 minutes, stirring occasionally.

Combine grits and cheese in a large mixing bowl; stir until cheese is melted. Combine eggs, milk, thyme, and garlic salt; mix well. Add a small amount of hot grits mixture to egg mixture, stirring well. Stir egg mixture into remaining grits mixture. Add cooked sausage, stirring well. Pour into a 12x8x2-inch baking dish. Cover and refrigerate overnight.

Remove from refrigerator; let stand 15 minutes. Bake at 350° for 50-55 minutes. Garnish with tomato roses and parsley.

Note: Recipe may be halved; bake at 350° in a 10x6x2-inch baking dish for 45 minutes.

Ham and Asparagus Quiche

Serves 6

9-inch deep dish pie crust
7 or 8 canned asparagus spears, drained
1 cup Swiss cheese, cubed small
¼ cup Parmesan cheese
½ cup chopped ham
2 cups half-and-half
3 eggs, beaten well
Dash of nutmeg

Preheat oven to 400°. Prick bottom of pie crust. Line crust bottom with ham. Top ham with cheese cubes. Sprinkle with Parmesan cheese. Mix together eggs and half-and-half; pour over ham and cheese. Place asparagus spears in a spoke pattern in the quiche. Sprinkle with nutmeg. Bake at 400° for 10 minutes, reduce heat to 350° and continue to bake for 35 minutes, until knife inserted in center comes out clean. Cool before cutting.

Upside-Down Orange Puffs

Yields 6 servings

2 tablespoons butter or margarine, melted
¼ cup sugar
3 tablespoons orange juice
1 teaspoon grated orange rind
1 (4.5-ounce) can refrigerated biscuit

Combine butter, sugar, orange juice, and orange rind, mixing well.

Pour about 1 tablespoon orange mixture in each cup of a 6-cup muffin pan. Place 1 biscuit in each cup. Bake at 400° for about 10 minutes. Invert pan on serving plate. Serve warm.

Hominy and Cheese Puff

Yields 4 servings

¾ cup hominy grits
1 cup boiling water
1½ teaspoon salt
2 cups milk
¼ cup butter or margarine
1 cup grated sharp cheddar cheese
4 eggs, separated

Cook hominy in boiling, salted water in top part of double boiler for 2 minutes, stirring constantly. Stir in milk and cook 30 minutes, stirring occasionally. Add butter and cheese; cook until cheese is melted. Add beaten egg yolks and fold in stiffly beaten egg whites. Bake in greased 1½-quart casserole in 350° oven for 45 minutes.

Cornmeal Puff

Yields 10-12 servings

1 cup of cornmeal
1½ teaspoons of salt
4 cups of milk
1 cup whipping cream
1 cup shredded Swiss cheese, divided
Fresh parsley sprigs

Combine cornmeal and salt in a medium saucepan; stir in milk. Bring to a boil; reduce heat and simmer, stirring occasionally, until thickened (about 4 minutes). Gradually add the whipping cream, stirring until smooth.

Spoon half of cornmeal mixture into a lightly greased 8-inch square baking dish. Sprinkle ½ cup cheese over top. Spoon remaining cornmeal mixture over cheese. Bake at 350° for 35 minutes. Sprinkle remaining cheese over casserole; bake 5 additional minutes. Garnish with parsley.

Note: Recipe can be doubled.

Harry Truman's Meatless Tuesday

Yields 4 to 6 servings

2 cups uncooked macaroni
4 tablespoons butter
2 tablespoons minced onions
4 tablespoons all-purpose flour
1 teaspoon salt
¾ teaspoon dry mustard
¼ teaspoon paprika
2 cups of milk
3 cups shredded cheddar cheese, divided
2 ripe tomatoes, blanched, peeled, and sliced into ½-inch thick slices

Preheat oven to 375°. Lightly grease a 13x9x2-inch baking dish.
Boil 6 cups of salted water, add macaroni, and cook al dente. Drain.
In a large saucepan, melt butter. Add onion and cook, stirring constantly, until tender. Add flour, salt, dry mustard, and paprika; mix well. Add milk and stir for 5 minutes, or until thickened. Add 2 cups shredded cheese and stir until melted. Stir in macaroni and pour into prepared dish. Cover macaroni with tomato slices and sprinkle with remaining cheese. Bake for 45-50 minutes.

Caramelized Onion Macaroni and Cheese

Yields 8 to 10 servings

1 (8 ounce) package large elbow macaroni
2 tablespoons butter
2 large onions, thinly sliced
1 teaspoon sugar
1 (16 ounce) block white cheddar cheese, shredded
1 cup (4 ounce) shredded Parmesan cheese
32 saltine crackers, finely crushed and divided
6 large eggs
4 cups of milk
1 teaspoon salt
½ teaspoon of pepper
2 tablespoons of butter, melted
½ cup chopped pecans (optional)

Prepare macaroni according to package directions, drain, and set aside. Melt 2 tablespoons of butter in a large skillet over medium-high heat. Add sliced onions and 1 teaspoon sugar. Cook, stirring often, 15-20 minutes or until onions are caramel colored. Layer half each of macaroni, onions, cheeses, and cracker crumbs in a lightly greased 13x9-inch baking dish. Layer with remaining macaroni, onions, and cheeses. Whisk together eggs and next 3 ingredients; pour over macaroni mixture. Stir together remaining cracker crumbs, melted butter, and if desired, pecans. Sprinkle evenly over macaroni mixture. Bake at 350° for 1 hour or until golden brown and set. Let stand 10 minutes before serving.

Lemon Linguine

Yields 4-6 servings

1 (8 ounce) package linguine
¼ cup minced onion or shallot
2 cloves garlic, crushed
1 tablespoon butter, melted
1 (8 ounce) carton sour cream
4 tablespoons freshly grated Parmesan cheese, divided
1 tablespoon milk
1½ teaspoons lemon pepper seasoning
¼ teaspoon of salt
1 tablespoon fresh lemon juice (about ½ medium lemon)
2 tablespoons chopped parsley
2 tablespoons of chives

Cook linguine, according to package directions. Drain and keep warm.

In a skillet, cook onion or shallots and garlic in butter, stirring constantly, until tender, not brown. Stir in sour cream, 2 tablespoons Parmesan cheese, milk, lemon pepper, salt, and lemon juice. Cook for about 1 minute. Remove from heat and pour over linguine. Toss gently, adding chopped parsley, chives, and remaining Parmesan cheese.

Chapter 5

Salads, Soups & Sauces

Easy Asparagus Salad

4 servings

1 pound fresh asparagus
Lettuce leaves
2 small tomatoes, sliced
2 hard-cooked eggs, sliced
1 small purple onion, sliced and separated into rings
Commercial ranch-style dressing

Snap off tough ends of asparagus and remove scales with a knife or vegetable peeler, if desired. Cook asparagus, covered, in a small amount of boiling water 6 to 8 minutes or until crisp-tender; drain. Chill 1 to 2 hours.
Line individual salad plates with lettuce leaves; arrange asparagus, tomato slices, egg slices, onion rings on top. Serve with ranch-style salad dressing.

Asparagus Vinaigrette

3 pounds fresh asparagus spears
1 sweet red pepper, cut into strips
1 tablespoon vegetable oil
¾ cup vegetable oil
¼ cup white vinegar
2 tablespoons water
1 tablespoon grated onion
1 teaspoon hot dry mustard
½ teaspoon salt
1 pinch of pepper

Snap off tough ends of asparagus. Remove scales from stalks with a knife or vegetable peeler, if desired. Cook asparagus, covered, in a small amount of boiling water 4 to 6 minutes or until crisp-tender. Drain. Rinse in cold water; drain.

Sauté red pepper in 1 tablespoon of oil until crisp-tender; drain. Cool strips.

Place asparagus and pepper strips in a 13x9 dish. Combine remaining ingredients; stir well, and pour over vegetables. Cover and chill at least 8 hours. Remove from marinade and serve.

BLT Salad with Warm Vinaigrette

Yields 4 servings

8 slices bacon
4 slices country Italian bread
1½ cups cherry tomatoes
8 cups romaine lettuce, torn
⅓ cup blue cheese crumbles
¼ cup cider vinegar
¼ cup olive oil
1 teaspoon sugar
1 teaspoon Dijon-style mustard
Salt and ground black pepper

In a large skillet, cook bacon over medium heat until crisp, turning occasionally. Remove bacon from skillet; drain on paper towels.

Meanwhile, toast bread. Halve cherry tomatoes. Break bacon in 2-inch pieces. On plates, layer toast, romaine, tomatoes, bacon, and blue cheese.

For vinaigrette, in screw-top jar, combine vinegar, oil, sugar, and mustard. Shake well. Season to taste with salt and pepper. Drizzle vinaigrette on salads.

Oriental Chicken Salad

Yields 4-5 servings

¼ cup soy sauce
2 tablespoons lemon juice
4 teaspoons sugar
1 tablespoon vegetable oil
2 teaspoons sesame seeds
1 teaspoon ground ginger
3 (5 ounce) cans boned chicken
1 (16 ounce) can bean sprouts, chilled, drained and rinsed
1 (6 ounce) can sliced bamboo shoots, drained
1 head iceburg lettuce
¼ cup finely shredded carrots

Mix all ingredients and chill at least 1 hour.

Hot Chicken Salad

3 cups chicken or turkey, cooked
2 cups packaged herb stuffing
¼ cup black olives, sliced
1 can bean sprouts
1 cup celery, chopped
2 tablespoons onion, chopped
1 cup salad dressing or mayonnaise
Salt and pepper to taste
⅔ cup margarine, melted
1 cup corn flakes, crushed

Combine cooked meat, stuffing mix, black olives, bean sprouts, chopped celery, onion, salad dressing, and salt and pepper to taste. Pour mixture into lightly greased baking dish. Combine melted margarine with crushed corn flakes. Sprinkle corn flake mixture over chicken salad. Bake at 375° for 20 minutes.

Creamy Chicken Salad

4 cups chicken, cooked, cooled and chopped
2 cups celery, chopped
4 tablespoons lemon juice
1 cup onion, chopped
1 (4 ounce) can mushrooms, drained
1 teaspoon salt
1 teaspoon Accent brand seasoning
1 cup almonds, slivered and toasted
1 cup mayonnaise
1 cup sour cream
1 cup American cheese, grated
2 cups potato chips, crushed

Combine chicken, celery, lemon juice, chopped onion, mushrooms, salt, Accent seasoning, almonds, sour cream and mayonnaise. Turn mixture into a lightly greased 9x13-inch baking dish. Mix grated cheese with crushed potato chips. Bake at 350° for 20 minutes.

Chicken Salad with Fruit

Yields 8-10 servings

4 cups chicken, cooked and chopped
2 cups celery, thinly sliced
1-2 tablespoons onion, minced
¾ cup mayonnaise
¼ cup whipping cream
1 tablespoon lemon juice
½ teaspoon salt
White pepper to taste
Lettuce leaves
¼ to ½ cup almonds, slivered and toasted
2-3 cups cantaloupe balls
Seedless green grapes

Combine chicken and celery. Combine next 6 ingredients, stirring well; add to chicken mixture, and toss well. Chill.

Serve salad on lettuce leaves. Sprinkle with toasted almonds, and garnish with melon balls and grapes.

Chicken-Avocado Salad

Yields 6 servings

1 medium-size ripe avocado, peeled and cubed
2-3 tablespoons lemon or lime juice
1 teaspoon salt
1 (3.5 ounce) can pitted ripe olives, drained and sliced
4-5 stalks celery, chopped (about 2 cups)
2 cups chicken, cooked and diced
½ cup mayonnaise
1 tablespoon lemon or lime juice
Lettuce leaves
3 hard-cooked eggs, quartered
Pimiento strips

Sprinkle avocado with 2 tablespoons lemon juice and salt; toss well.

Combine avocado, olives, celery, and chicken; stir gently. Combine mayonnaise and 1 tablespoon lemon or lime juice; mix well. Stir mayonnaise mixture into chicken mixture. Serve salad on lettuce; garnish with egg quarters and pimiento strips.

Chicken and Strawberry Salad

Yields 6 servings

½ cup poppy seed dressing
¼ cup mayonnaise
1½ pounds chicken, cooked and chopped (about 3 ½ cups)
2 celery ribs, sliced
1 pint fresh strawberries, halved
1 avocado, cut into 1-inch cubes
½ small red onion, thinly sliced
½ cup almonds, slivered and toasted
1 (10 ounce) package mixed salad greens
Garnishes: Avocado slices, whole strawberries

Whisk together dressing and mayonnaise in a large bowl; cover and chill 30 minutes.

Add chopped chicken and next 5 ingredients to dressing mixture, gently tossing to coat. Serve over mixed salad greens. Garnish, if desired.

Pineapple-Chicken Salad Pie

Yields 6 servings

1 (20 ounce) can pineapple chunks, drained
3 cups cooked chicken, diced
1 cup celery, chopped
¼ cup green onion, finely chopped
2 tablespoons lemon juice
1½ to 2 teaspoons seasoned salt
¼ cup cashew nuts, chopped
½ cup mayonnaise
1 baked 9-inch pastry shell, cooled

Combine half of pineapple chunks and next 7 ingredients; stir well. Spoon salad into pastry shell, pressing firmly. Garnish with remaining pineapple chunks; chill before serving.

Note: Pastry shell may be omitted; serve in lettuce.

Perfection Salad

2 envelopes Knox Gelatin
½ cup sugar
1 teaspoon salt
1½ cups water, boiling
1½ cups cold water or pineapple juice and water
2 cups finely shredded cabbage
1 cup celery
¼ cup pimiento
1 cup olives, sliced
1 (16 ounce) can crushed pineapple, drained

Stir gelatin, sugar, and salt until dissolved into boiling water. Add 1-½ cups cold water or pineapple juice and water. Chill until begins to thicken. Add cabbage, celery, pimiento, olives, crushed pineapple.

Note: Mold if desired and chill overnight.

Cranberry-Apple Mold

Yields 8 servings

1 (3 ounce) package raspberry-flavored gelatin
¾ cup boiling water
1 (8 ounce) can crushed pineapple, drained
1 (16 ounce) can whole-berry cranberry sauce
1 Red Delicious apple, unpeeled and coarsely grated
1 tablespoon grated orange rind
⅛ teaspoon salt
⅛ teaspoon ground cinnamon
Dash of ground cloves
Lettuce leaves
Garnishes: Fresh cranberries and orange rind strips

Dissolve raspberry-flavored gelatin in boiling water, and let cool. Stir in next 7 ingredients, and spoon into a lightly oiled 4-cup mold. Cover and chill until firm.

Unmold on lettuce leaves. Garnish, if desired.

Holiday Salad

Yields 8 servings

½ cup cold water
2 envelopes plain gelatin
½ cup champagne vinegar or white vinegar
1 cup granulated sugar
1 teaspoon kosher salt
3 cups peeled and seeded cucumbers, cut in ¼-inch pieces
½ cup thinly sliced green onions, white and green parts
½ cup celery, cut into ¼-inch pieces
Vegetable oil or cooking spray

In a bowl, pour ½ cup cold water. Sprinkle gelatin over water to soften about 10 minutes. In a nonreactive saucepan, combine 1 cup water, vinegar, sugar, and salt. Cook and stir over medium heat until hot and sugar is dissolved. Remove from heat; add softened gelatin mixture, stirring until dissolved. Transfer to a large bowl.

Place bowl over a very large bowl of ice water. Stir occasionally until completely cold and just beginning to thicken, about 10 minutes.

Stir cucumbers, green onions, and celery into cold mixture. Pour into 6 to 8 cup nonreactive mold or dish that has been lightly oiled. Wrap mold with plastic wrap; refrigerate 4 hours or overnight.

To unmold, dip mold briefly (10 seconds or less) in hot water. Invert mold onto a serving dish.

Lime Gelatin Salad

Yields 12 servings

1 (6 ounce) package lime Jell-O
1 (8 ounce) package cream cheese
1 (8 ounce) carton of Cool Whip
1½ cups boiling water
1½ cups crushed pineapple, undrained

Pour 1 cup boiling water over the Jell-O in a large bowl and stir until dissolved. Add ½ cup pineapple juice. Place in refrigerator to partially gel. It is important that it is partially gelled.

When the salad is partially gelled, blend the soft cream cheese into it until it is creamy. Mix in the pineapple and Cool Whip and place in 9x13 pan in refrigerator.

Green Jell-O Salad

Yields 12 servings

½ cup sugar
1 (6 ounce) package lime Jell-O
1 cup boiling water
2 tablespoons fresh lemon juice
1 (8 ounce) can crushed pineapple
2 cups heavy cream

Put sugar, Jell-O, and boiling water into a medium bowl, stir until dissolved (about 2-3 minutes). Add lemon juice and pineapple. Stir well and refrigerate until mixture has a syrupy consistency (about 45-50 minutes). Whip heavy cream until stiff peaks form, then gently fold the cream into the Jell-O mixture. Transfer the mixture into a 9x13 pan, smooth the top with a spatula, and refrigerate until firm. Serve chilled.

24 Hour Salad

1 large can white cherries, seeded and cut in half
1 large can pineapple tidbits
24 marshmallows, cut into small pieces
2 oranges
1 cup cream
4 egg yolks
Juice of 1 lemon
Pinch of salt
1 pint whipped cream

Mix cherries, pineapple tidbits, marshmallows and oranges. Drain well. In a double boiler, cook cream, egg yolks and lemon juice until it becomes thick. Let cool and fold the whipped cream into cooled custard. Then add other mixture. Place in a large bowl and refrigerate for 24 hours. Serve on lettuce, (it will be light and fluffy).

Swan's Nest Leaf Lettuce with Poppy Seed Dressing

Yields 4 servings

1 teaspoon dry mustard
1 teaspoon salt
1 tablespoon poppy seeds
¾ cup sugar
½ cup apple cider vinegar
1 cup salad oil
1 head red leaf lettuce, washed, drained and torn into bite-size pieces
1 head green leaf lettuce, washed, drained and torn into bite-size pieces
1 cup strawberries, sliced
1 cup canned mandarin oranges

Mix dry mustard, salt, poppy seeds and sugar. Then add salad oil and then vinegar. Mix well and chill. To serve, assemble lettuce, strawberries and mandarin oranges in a bowl and pour dressing over salad.

Frozen Fruit Salad

Yields 4-6 servings

1 (3 ounce) package cream cheese
2 tablespoons cream
⅓ cup mayonnaise
2 tablespoons lemon juice
Salt to taste
1 cup diced pineapple
½ cup chopped pecans
½ cup maraschino cherries, chopped
1 cup orange, sliced
2 tablespoons sugar
1 cup whipped cream

Mix cream cheese thoroughly with 2 tablespoons cream. Add mayonnaise, lemon juice, and salt. Mix well. Add pineapple, pecans, cherries, oranges, and sugar; mix well. Whip cream and fold into mixture. Pour into freezing tray and allow to freeze without stirring. Cut into squares and serve on lettuce leaves.

Frozen Cranberry Salad

Yields 8-10 servings

2 (3 ounce) packages cream cheese
2 tablespoons mayonnaise
2 tablespoons sugar
1 (8 ounce) can crushed pineapple
1 (16 ounce) can whole cranberry sauce
½ cup pecans, chopped
½ whipping cream, whipped

Mix first four ingredients and add cranberry sauce and pecans. Fold in whipping cream. Freeze in individual molds or ice tray.

Ham Loaf Salad

Yields 8-10 servings

4 cups ground cooked ham
1 cup celery, chopped
1 cup crackers, crushed
½ cup salad dressing
4 envelopes unflavored gelatin
½ cup cold water
1 (4 ounce) can pimientos, chopped
1 medium green pepper, chopped
1 tablespoon freshly squeezed lemon juice
3 hard-cooked eggs, chopped
Salad greens

Combine ham, celery, crackers, and salad dressing. Sprinkle gelatin over cold water and heat until dissolved. Stir into ham mixture. Add pimientos, green pepper, lemon juice, and chopped eggs. Blend well and press mixture into a 1½ quart oblong dish; chill until firm. Slice and serve on salad greens.

Crab Classic Salad with Lemon & Parsley

Yields 2-3 servings

8 ounce crab classic
2 tablespoons light sour cream
2 tablespoons light mayonnaise
2 teaspoons lemon juice
2 tablespoons parsley, chopped
4 tablespoons red onion, small diced
4 tablespoons celery, small diced

Combine all of the ingredients. Mix well. Season with salt and pepper to taste. Serve over mixed greens.

Tuna Almondine

Yields 5½ cups

2 envelopes unflavored gelatin
½ cup cold water
1 cup boiling water
2 (8 ounce) packages cream cheese
2 tablespoons lemon juice
1 tablespoon curry powder
½ to 1 teaspoon salt
¼ teaspoon garlic powder
⅓ cup green onions, finely chopped
1 (2 ounce) jar pimientos, chopped
2 (7 ounce) cans tuna, drained and flaked
1¼ cups almonds, sliced and lightly toasted

In a large bowl, sprinkle unflavored gelatin over cold water; let stand for 1 minute. Add boiling water and stir until gelatin is completely dissolved. With wire whip or rotary beater, blend in cream cheese until smooth. Stir in lemon juice, curry powder, salt and garlic powder. Fold in green onions, pimiento, tuna and ½ cup almonds. Turn into 5½ cup mold or bowl; chill until firm. To serve, unmold onto platter. Garnish with remaining almonds, overlapping to form scales; and if desired, green olive slices, parsley and pimiento strips. Serve with crackers or party breads.

Curried Salmon Pasta Salad

Yields 8 servings

1 cup dry pasta, such as macaroni or small shells
8 ounces cooked, skinned salmon or 7½ ounce can red salmon,
cut into chunks
½ cup red or yellow onion, minced
1 cup celery, diced
1 medium to large apple, diced
½ cup chopped walnuts or dry-roasted unsalted peanuts

Dressing:
6 ounce (¾ cup) fat-free yogurt
2 tablespoons olive oil
1 tablespoon curry powder
2 teaspoons fresh lemon juice
2 garlic cloves, crushed
1 teaspoon Dijon mustard
½ teaspoon salt (or to taste)
Freshly ground black pepper to taste

Cook pasta per package directions; drain and rinse. In a large bowl combine first six ingredients. In a small bowl, combine dressing ingredients. Pour dressing over salad; toss. Refrigerate or serve at room temperature.

Garden-Fresh Taco Salad

Yields 4 servings

1 pound ground beef
1 envelope taco seasoning, divided in half
1 large head lettuce, shredded
4 medium tomatoes, seeded and diced
1 medium onion, chopped
2 cups shredded cheddar cheese
1 cup mayonnaise or salad dressing
1 tablespoon salsa
Leaf lettuce
Tortilla chips, crushed

In a skillet, cook beef over medium heat until no longer pink; drain. Stir in half of the taco seasoning. Remove from heat; stir in shredded lettuce, tomatoes, onion and cheese. In a small bowl, combine mayonnaise, salsa and remaining taco seasoning. Pour over salad and toss to coat. Line a large bowl or platter with leaf lettuce; top with taco salad. Sprinkle tortilla chips around edge.

Fiesta Salad

Yields 8 servings

1 pound lean ground beef
1 pound ground pork
¾ cup water
½ (2 ounce) package onion soup-and-dip mix
1 tablespoon chili powder
2 large ripe avocados
1 (8 ounce) container French onion dip
1½ teaspoons lemon juice
1 (9 ounce) bag tortilla chips, divided
2 (5 ounce) packages mixed salad greens
1 (12 ounce) jar chunky salsa
1 cup (4 ounce) shredded cheddar cheese
1 (2.25 ounce) can sliced ripe black olives, drained
Garnish: Tomato wedges

Cook ground beef and pork in a large skillet over medium-high heat, stirring until meat crumbles and is no longer pink; drain and return to skillet. Stir in water, onion soup mix, and chili powder; reduce heat, and simmer for 6 to 7 minutes or until liquid evaporates. Remove from heat, and set aside.

Cut avocados in half. Scoop pulp into a bowl; mash with a fork just until slightly chunky. Stir in onion dip and lemon juice. Coarsely crush half of tortilla chips.

Spread crushed chips evenly in 8 serving dishes; top with salad greens, meat mixture, and avocado mixture. Spoon ¼ cup of salsa onto each salad, and sprinkle evenly with cheese and olives. Garnish, if desired. Serve immediately with remaining half of chips.

Crunchy Romaine Salad

1 large head of Romaine lettuce or 1 bag of Italian blend mixed greens
2 cups broccoli florets
3 green onions
1 package of Ramen noodles
1 cup English walnuts or pecans
1 tablespoon of butter

Dressing:
1 cup sugar
½ cup vinegar
3 tablespoons soy sauce
¾ cup vegetable oil
Salt and pepper to taste

In a large bowl, combine lettuce, broccoli, and onions. Break up Ramen noodles and nuts; brown in butter over medium heat, stirring constantly. When brown, drain on paper towel. In a blender combine sugar, vinegar, soy sauce, salt, and pepper. Gradually add oil in a thin stream and blend well. Add Ramen noodles and nuts to salad mixture and pour dressing over salad.

Note: This is a popular salad recipe provided by Barbara Hunt.

Thai Cucumber Salad

Yields 4 servings

¼ cup sugar
1 teaspoon salt
½ cup rice vinegar
4 pickling or slicing cucumbers, sliced lengthwise, seeded and thinly sliced
1 shallot, thinly sliced
10 whole cilantro leaves
¼ cup red pepper, julienned

Combine the sugar, vinegar and salt and heat in a small saucepan until sugar has dissolved (approximately 5 minutes); do not boil. Set saucepan in cold water to cool the vinegar mixture. When cool, pour over cucumbers and garnish with red peppers.

Marinated Mixed Vegetables

14 servings

1 pound fresh broccoli, cut into florets
1 large head of cauliflower, cut into florets
2 yellow squash, cut into thin strips
2 cups sliced carrots
1 large green pepper, cut into thin strips

Dressing:
¾ cup vegetable oil
¼ cup plus 2 tablespoons red wine vinegar
2 teaspoons sugar
1 teaspoon salt
1 teaspoon dry mustard
1 teaspoon dried whole basil
½ teaspoon pepper
⅛ teaspoon ground nutmeg
2 cloves garlic, crushed

Combine broccoli, cauliflower, squash, carrots, green pepper in a bowl. In a jar, combine all of the dressing ingredients. Cover tightly, and shake mixture vigorously. Pour dressing over vegetables; toss gently. Cover and chill for 8 hours. Drain vegetables before serving.

Cucumbers in Sour Cream

2 cucumbers
1 teaspoon salt
2 teaspoon sugar
1 teaspoon grated onion
2 tablespoon wine vinegar
2 tablespoon snipped dill
1 cup sour cream

Mix sour cream in a bowl with vinegar, salt, sugar, onion and dill. Taste to see if it is too sweet or too sharp. Slice unpeeled cucumbers and add to sauce. Let marinate a few hours before serving.

Cool Cabbage Salad

Yields 6 servings

1 small green cabbage (1½ pounds)
3 medium-sized carrots, pared, halved, chopped (¾ cup)
1 large sweet green pepper, halved, seeded, and chopped (¾ cup)
1 large sweet red pepper, halved, seeded, and chopped (¾ cup)
1 small cucumber, chopped (¾ cup)
1 large bunch radishes, chopped (about ¾ cup)
1 large onion, chopped (¾ cup)
1 cup plus 2 tablespoons white vinegar
¾ cup vegetable oil
¾ cup sugar
1 teaspoon salt
¼ teaspoon pepper

Trim outer leaves from cabbage; reserve 4 attractive outer leaves; refrigerate. Quarter, core, and shred remaining cabbage (should yield approximately 6 cups). Combine shredded cabbage, carrot, celery, green pepper, red pepper, cucumber, radish and onion in a large bowl. Combine vinegar, oil, sugar, salt, and pepper in a screw-top jar; cover; shake well to blend. Pour dressing over cabbage mixture; toss to coat. Cover and refrigerate for several hours. To serve, line a salad bowl with the reserved 4 outer leaves. Toss cabbage mixture; mound into a salad bowl. Garnish with a radish rose, cucumber slices and radish slices, if you wish.

Cherry Tomato-Cucumber Salad

Yields 6 servings

1 pint cherry tomatoes, halved
1 medium cucumber, peeled, seeded, and thinly sliced
¼ cup thinly sliced sweet onion
¼ cup chopped fresh parsley
2 tablespoons olive oil
1 tablespoon lemon juice
1 teaspoon salt
½ teaspoon pepper

Toss together all ingredients in a medium bowl to combine.

Wilted Salad Greens

4 servings

1 cup thinly sliced Vidalia or other sweet onion
3 tablespoons olive oil
½ cup pecan halves
2 tablespoons red wine vinegar
2 tablespoons honey
10 cups mixed greens
Salt and cracked pepper to taste

Sauté onion slices in hot oil in a medium skillet over medium heat 6 minutes or until tender and golden brown. Add pecans, and cook 2 minutes or until pecans are lightly toasted. Stir in vinegar and honey; remove from heat. Toss together salad greens and warm onion mixture in a large salad bowl just until greens are thoroughly warmed. Sprinkle with salt and pepper to taste.

Sweet-Sour Slaw

8 servings

1 large head cabbage, coarsely shredded
1 green pepper, finely chopped
1 medium onion, finely chopped
1 cup sugar
1 cup vinegar
¾ cup vegetable oil
1 tablespoon salt
1 teaspoon celery salt
1 teaspoon mustard seeds

Combine shredded cabbage, green pepper, and onion in a large bowl. Sprinkle with sugar. Combine remaining ingredients in a small saucepan; bring to a boil. Pour over cabbage mixture; cover and refrigerate at least 4 hours. Toss before serving.

Green Wonder Salad

3 pints

1 can French-style green beans
1 can small English peas
1 can fancy Chinese vegetables, without meat
1 (6 ounce) can water chestnuts, thinly sliced
1½ cups of thinly sliced celery
3 medium onions, thinly sliced
1 cup sugar
¾ cup cider vinegar
1 teaspoon salt
Pepper to taste

Drain and discard liquid from all canned vegetables. Mix all ingredients in a large bowl. Cover and refrigerate for several hours or overnight before serving. This will keep several weeks in the refrigerator if container is tightly covered.

Layered Lettuce Salad

1 small head lettuce
1 cup celery, diced
4 hard-cooked eggs, sliced
1 (10 ounce) package frozen peas, uncooked
½ cup green pepper, diced
1 medium sweet onion, diced
8-10 slices of bacon, fried crisp and crumbled
2 cups mayonnaise or Miracle Whip
2 tablespoons sugar
6-8 ounces cheddar cheese, grated

Tear clean lettuce into bite-size pieces and place into a 9x13x2-inch baking dish or large salad bowl. Layer the rest of the ingredients in the order given. Combine the sugar and the mayonnaise or salad dressing and spread on top as you would frosting. Top with grated cheese. Cover and refrigerate for 8-10 hours or overnight. May garnish with parsley or additional bacon.

Marinated Tomatoes

6-8 servings

¾ cup vegetable oil
½ cup red wine vinegar
3 tablespoons chopped fresh parsley
1 tablespoon sugar
1½ teaspoons garlic salt
1½ teaspoons seasoned salt
¾ teaspoon dried oregano
½ teaspoon pepper
10 plum tomatoes (about 2½ pounds)

Combine vegetable oil and next 7 ingredients in a large zip-top plastic freezer bag. Core and cut each tomato into 4 wedges; add to marinade in plastic bag. Seal and shake to coat tomato wedges. Chill 4 hours; let stand 30 minutes at room temperature before serving. Serve with a slotted spoon.

Corn Salad

9 servings

¼ cup lime juice
1 tablespoon honey
1 jalapeno pepper, seeded and finely chopped
3 tablespoons snipped fresh mint
¼ teaspoon salt
6 fresh ears of corn, husked and cleaned or 3 cups frozen whole kernel corn, thawed
1½ cups baby spinach leaves
1 large tomato, seeded and chopped
¾ cup seeded and chopped cucumber

In a large bowl whisk together lime juice and honey until well combined. Stir in jalapeno pepper, cilantro, and salt. Carefully cut corn kernels off cobs. Add to lime juice mixture. Stir in spinach, tomato, and cucumber. Serve immediately.

Amish Vegetable Salad

1 can sliced carrots
1 can green beans
1 jar diced pimiento
1 can corn
1 can green peas
1 cup sugar
1 teaspoon salt
1 teaspoon pepper
½ cup oil
½ cup vinegar
1 cup celery, chopped
1 green pepper, chopped
¾ cup green onions, chopped

In a bowl, combine carrots, green beans, diced pimiento, corn and green peas. Drain well and set aside. Mix sugar, salt, pepper, oil, and vinegar and bring to a boil. Cool and set aside. Mix celery, green peppers, and green onions with drained vegetables. Add other mixture and let set for 4 hours before serving. This is best if made the day before.

Poppy Seed Dressing for Fruit Salad

1½ cups sugar
2 teaspoons dry mustard
2 teaspoons salt
⅔ cups of vinegar
3 tablespoons onion juice
2 cups salad oil
3 tablespoons poppy seeds

Mix sugar, mustard, salt and vinegar. Add onion juice and stir thoroughly. Add oil and heat consistently and continue to heat until thick. Add poppy seeds and use or store in a cold place.

Fruit Salad Dressing

3 eggs (¾ cup), slightly beaten
¼ cup orange juice
¼ cup lemon juice
¼ cup unsweetened pineapple juice
1 cup sugar
2 tablespoons flour
½ cup whipping cream, whipped

Blend the first four ingredients together in top of a double broiler. Add a mixture of the sugar and flour gradually to the egg mixture, stirring constantly. Cook over simmering water, stirring constantly, until thick (about 10 minutes). Cool and chill. Blend chilled mixture into whipped cream just before serving.

Honey-Mustard Dressing

Yields 1¾ cups

1 cup mayonnaise
3 tablespoons yellow mustard
3 tablespoons honey
2 tablespoons chopped fresh basil
2 tablespoons vegetable oil
2 teaspoons cider vinegar
½ teaspoon minced garlic
¼ teaspoon ground red pepper

Whisk together all ingredients; cover and chill at least 4 hours.

Autumn Soup

2 pounds ground beef
2 cups chopped onion
2 quarts hot water
2 cups cut-up carrots
2 cups cut-up celery
2 cups cut-up potatoes
3 teaspoons salt
1 teaspoon pepper
2 teaspoons instant beef bouillon
2 bay leaves, crumbled
Pinch of basil
1 (28 ounce) can of tomatoes

Brown the ground beef. Add chopped onion and cook 5 minutes more; drain. Add water, vegetables, salt, pepper, beef bouillon, bay leaves, basil, and tomatoes. Cook until vegetables are tender.

Mexican Chili

Yields 7 cups

2 pounds ground beef
¾ cup chopped green pepper
1 cup chopped onion
1 clove garlic, minced
1 (16 ounce) can kidney beans, drained
2 (8 ounce) cans tomato sauce
1 (16 ounce) can tomatoes, undrained and chopped
1 fresh or canned green chile, seeded and chopped
1 tablespoon plus 1 teaspoon chili powder
2 teaspoons ground cumin
½ teaspoon dried whole basil
½ teaspoon salt
¼ teaspoon pepper
¼ teaspoon hot sauce
Shredded Cheddar cheese (optional)
Corn chips (optional)

Combine first 4 ingredients in a Dutch oven; cook over medium heat until meat is browned, stirring to crumble meat. Drain off drippings. Add kidney beans and next 9 ingredients; cover, reduce heat, and simmer 20 minutes, stirring occasionally. If desired, serve with shredded Cheddar cheese and corn chips.

Sunday Stew

Yields 4 servings

1 pound cubed beef
1 cup peas
1 cup sliced carrots
1 chopped onion
1 large potato cubed
1 teaspoon salt
½ teaspoon pepper
1 can cream of mushroom soup
½ soup can water

Mix all ingredients. Put in large casserole with tight fitting lid. Cook at 275º for 5 hours.

Best Bean Soup

Yields 2 ½ quarts

1 package 10 Bean Soup Mix (2 cups)
2 tablespoons salt
8 cups water
8 ounces country ham pieces
1 medium onion, chopped
1 (28 ounce) can tomatoes, cut up
1 clove garlic, minced
1 teaspoon chili powder
Juice of 1 lemon
Salt and pepper to taste

10 Bean Soup

Black turtle beans
Pinto beans
Black-eyed peas
Navy beans
Lentils
Great Northern Beans
Kidney Beans
Small lima beans
Barley
Idaho red beans
Split peas

Wash beans thoroughly and place in large kettle. Cover with water 2-inches above beans, add 2 tablespoons salt and soak overnight.

The next morning drain beans, return to kettle and add 8 cups fresh water. Add country ham pieces, onions, tomatoes and their juice, garlic, and lemon juice. Cover and bring to boil; reduce heat and simmer for 3 hours or until beans are tender, stirring occasionally. Add salt and pepper to taste and cook 30 minutes longer. Enjoy. Serve with corn bread and green salad for a great cold weather meal!

Bean Soup

3 (15½ ounce) cans great northern beans, undrained
1 (15½ ounce) can hominy, undrained
1 (14½ ounce) can stewed tomatoes, undrained
1 (11½ ounce) can bean with bacon soup, undrained
1 (10 ounce) can dried Rotel with green chilies, undrained
1 (11 ounce) can whole kernel yellow corn, undrained
2 cups water
2 bay leaves
1 tablespoon cilantro or dried parsley
1 teaspoon cumin
Sharp Cheddar cheese

Combine first 10 ingredients and bring to a boil; cover and reduce heat. Simmer for 30 minutes. Discard bay leaf or leaves. Sprinkle each serving with sharp cheddar cheese.

Note: Freezes well.

Curried Pumpkin Soup

Yields 7 servings

½ pound fresh mushrooms, sliced
½ cup chopped onion
2 tablespoons butter or margarine
2 tablespoons all-purpose flour
½ to 1 teaspoon curry powder
3 cups vegetable broth
1 (15 ounce) can solid-packed pumpkin
1 (12 ounces) can evaporated milk
1 tablespoon honey
½ teaspoon salt
¼ teaspoon pepper
¼ teaspoon ground nutmeg
Fresh or frozen chives (optional)

In a large saucepan, sauté the mushrooms and onion in butter until tender. Stir in the flour and curry powder until blended. Gradually add the broth. Bring to a boil; cook and stir for 2 minutes or until thickened. Add the pumpkin, milk, honey, salt, pepper, and nutmeg; heat through. Garnish with chives if desired.

Baked Potato Soup

Yields 12 cups

5 large baking potatoes, baked
¼ cup butter or margarine
1 medium onion, chopped
⅓ cup all-purpose flour
1 quart half-and-half
3 cups milk
1 teaspoon salt
⅛ teaspoon ground white pepper
2 cups shredded cheddar cheese
8 bacon slices, cooked and crumbled

In order to bake potatoes in microwave, prick each several times with a fork. Microwave 1-inch apart on paper towels on high for 14 minutes or until done, turning and rearranging after 5 minutes.

Peel potatoes, and coarsely mash with a fork.

Melt butter in a Dutch oven over medium heat; add onion, and sauté until tender. Add flour, stirring until smooth. Stir in potatoes, half-and-half, and next 3 ingredients; cook over low heat until thoroughly heated. Top each serving with cheese and bacon.

Mushroom-Artichoke Soup

Yields 10 servings

1 pound fresh mushrooms sliced
1 pound fresh shitake mushrooms, stemmed and sliced
1 cup thinly sliced shallots
2 large carrots, sliced
¼ cup butter
3 tablespoons all-purpose flour
½ teaspoon dried thyme, crushed
½ teaspoon garlic powder
¼ teaspoon crushed red pepper (optional)
2 (14 ounce) cans chicken broth
2 (14 ounce) cans artichoke hearts, drained and quartered
¼ cup oil-packed dried tomatoes; drained and chopped
1 bay leaf
1 cup half-and-half or light cream
Green onions, cut in thin strips

In a 5½ to 6 quart Dutch oven cook mushrooms; shallots, and carrots in hot butter for about 15 minutes or until mushrooms are tender; stir occasionally. Stir in flour, thyme, garlic powder, ½ teaspoon each salt and pepper if desired, and if desired, crushed red peppers. Add broth all at once. Cook and stir until soup is slightly thickened and bubbly.

Stir in artichoke, tomatoes, and bay leaf. Simmer, covered, for 15 minutes. Stir in half-and-half; heat through. Discard bay leaf. Top with green onions.

Orange Sauce

1½ cups sugar
1 large orange, squeezed
1 lemon, squeezed

Grate the rind of each fruit, and cook all ingredients in a double boiler until the sauce is thick. Good served over melon and fresh fruit.

Cucumber Sauce

Yields about 1½ cups
½ cup peeled, chopped cucumber
½ cup mayonnaise
½ cup commercial sour cream
1 tablespoon chopped chives
½ teaspoon chopped fresh parsley
¼ teaspoon salt
¼ teaspoon dried dillweed

Combine all ingredients; mix well and chill. Serve with seafood.

Cranberry-Orange Sauce

1 can cranberry sauce
¾ cup chopped onions
1 cup orange juice
¼ teaspoon cinnamon
¼ teaspoon ginger

Combine all ingredients, and baste pork roast with sauce.

Raisin Sauce for Ham

Yields 2 cups

½ cup packed brown sugar
2 tablespoons cornstarch
1 teaspoon ground mustard
1½ cups water
½ cup raisins
2 tablespoons white vinegar
2 tablespoons lemon juice
¼ teaspoon grated lemon peel
2 tablespoons butter or margarine

In a saucepan, combine brown sugar, cornstarch, and mustard. Stir in the water, raisins, vinegar, lemon juice and peel, until blended. Bring to a boil; cook and stir for 2 minutes or until thickened. Stir in butter until melted. Serve warm over sliced ham.

Cocktail Sauce

Yields about 1¼ cups

1 cup bottled chili sauce
¼ cup prepared horseradish
1 tablespoon fresh lemon juice
1 teaspoon bottled hot pepper sauce (optional)

In a small bowl combine chili sauce, horseradish, lemon juice, and hot pepper sauce. Season to taste with salt and black pepper. Store, refrigerated, up to 1 week.

Chapter 6

Main Course Dishes:
Stir Fry, Casseroles, Seafood,
Chicken, Ham, Pork & Beef

Stir-Fry Chicken

Yields 4 servings about 285 calories each
3 tablespoons soy sauce, divided
2 tablespoons plus 2 teaspoons dry sherry, divided
12 ounces skinless, boneless chicken breasts, cut into 1-inch pieces
3 tablespoons salad oil, divided
6 ounces snow peas, cut into 1-inch slices
1 cup red pepper, cut into 1-inch squares
8 asparagus spears, cut into 2-inch slices
½ cup sliced water chestnuts
2 teaspoons finely chopped garlic
1 to 1½ teaspoons finely chopped ginger
2 tablespoons water
1 tablespoon sugar
2 teaspoons wine vinegar
2 teaspoons cornstarch
¼ to ½ teaspoons red pepper flakes
1 tablespoon sesame oil

In a small bowl, combine 1 tablespoon soy sauce and 2 teaspoons dry sherry. Toss in chicken. In skillet heat 1 tablespoon salad oil. Add vegetables and water chestnuts; stir to coat with oil. Cover; cook 1 minute. Uncover and cook, string 1 minute. Remove from skillet.

To same skillet add remaining oil. Add chicken; stir-fry quickly, about 2 minutes. Add garlic and ginger; cook 1 minute. In small bowl combine remaining soy sauce and dry sherry with next 5 ingredients.

Return vegetables to skillet; turn heat to high. Add sauce. Cook, stirring constantly, until sauce thickens. Sprinkle with sesame oil.

Stir-Fry of Chicken with Orange and Pea Pods

Yields 4 servings

3 tablespoons dry sherry
2 tablespoons cornstarch
1 egg white
3 (4 to a pound) boneless, skinless chicken breasts, cut in ¾-inch cubes
Juice and minced peel of 1 small orange
½ cup chicken broth
2 tablespoons soy sauce
1 cup oil
3 cloves of garlic, peeled and minced
1 jalapeno chili, seeded and minced
1 teaspoon minced ginger
¼ cup chopped water chestnuts
16 Chinese pea pods, cut in halves diagonally
4 oven-fried noodle nests (recipe below), or hot cooked rice

In bowl, beat 1 tablespoon sherry, 1 tablespoon cornstarch and egg white until light and frothy. Add chicken pieces and mix to coat thoroughly. Set aside.

In measuring cup or small bowl, combine remaining sherry and cornstarch. Stir in orange juice, chicken broth and soy sauce. Set aside.

Heat wok over medium heat. Add oil and heat 30 seconds. Add half of chicken and cook, stirring to break apart pieces. Cook, stirring frequently just until chicken turns opaque, about 2 minutes. Remove from pan with slotted spoon and set aside. Repeat with remaining chicken.

Discard all but 2 tablespoons oil. Add garlic, jalapeno, ginger, and orange peel to pan. Cook about 10 seconds. Return chicken to wok along with water chestnuts and peas and stir fry 1 minute. Stir orange juice mixture and add to pan. Bring to boil and cook, stirring until sauce thickens and turns clear.

Serve immediately over noodle nest or rice.

Oven-Fried Noodle Nests

Yields 4 servings

8 ounces Chinese egg noodles, cooked and drained
1 tablespoon oil
¼ teaspoon salt

Allow noodles to drain thoroughly or pat with paper towels to absorb excess moisture. Toss with oil and salt. Coil noodles into 4 nests on baking sheet. Bake at 375° for minutes. Turn and bake 10-15 minutes longer or until lightly browned and crisp on outside but still soft on inside.

Spicy Beef and Vegetable Stir-Fry

Yields 4 servings

½ cup low-sodium beef broth
1 tablespoon reduced-sodium soy sauce
2 teaspoons cornstarch
1 teaspoon Dijon mustard
6 broccoli spears
2 teaspoons peanut oil
1 cup cauliflower florets
½ cup chopped onion
1 clove garlic, finely chopped
8 ounces cooked lean roast beef, cut into strips
1 ounce unsalted peanuts, coarsely chopped
¼ teaspoon red pepper flakes
¼ teaspoon freshly ground black pepper

In a small bowl, combine the beef broth, soy sauce, cornstarch, and mustard, and stir until the cornstarch is dissolved. Set aside.

Cut the broccoli into bite-size pieces.

In a nonstick wok or large nonstick skillet, warm the oil over medium-high heat until hot but not smoking. Add the broccoli, cauliflower, onion, and garlic, and stir-fry until the vegetables are crisp-tender and the onion begins to brown, 4 to 5 minutes.

Stir the cornstarch mixture again and pour it into the wok. Stir in the beef, peanuts, red pepper flakes, and black pepper, and stir-fry until the sauce thickens and the beef is heated through, 2 to 3 minutes. If necessary, reduce the heat to keep the sauce from evaporating.

Stir Fried Vegetables

Yields 6 servings

1 tablespoon butter or margarine, melted
1 tablespoon soy sauce
1 (6 ounce) package frozen Chinese pea pods, thawed
2 stalks celery, sliced
2 carrots, sliced thin diagonally
1 green pepper, sliced thin
1 green onion, chopped
2 cup broccoli florets

In a 3-quart casserole, toss all ingredients. Cover tightly with plastic wrap. Microwave on high 4 minutes. Stir well.

Five-Veggie Stir-Fry

Yields 4 servings

2 tablespoons cornstarch
2 tablespoons sugar
½ teaspoon ground ginger
1 cup orange juice
¼ cup reduced-sodium soy sauce
2 garlic cloves, minced
2 large carrots, sliced
2 cups of broccoli florets
2 cups cauliflower
4 teaspoons olive or canola oil, divided
1 cup quartered fresh mushrooms
1 cup fresh or frozen snow peas
4 cups hot cooked rice

In a small bowl, combine the cornstarch, sugar and ginger. Stir in orange juice, soy sauce, and garlic until blended; set aside. In a nonstick skillet or wok, stir-fry the carrots, broccoli, and cauliflower in 3 teaspoons of oil for 4-5 minutes. Add mushrooms, peas and remaining oil; stir-fry for 3 minutes. Stir orange juice mixture and add to the pan. Bring to a boil; cook and stir until thickened. Serve over rice.

Stir-Fried Shrimp with Snow Peas

Yields 4 servings

¾ pound medium shrimp, such as Gulf of Mexico
white, peeled, deveined, and halved lengthwise
1 ½ tablespoons salt
2½ tablespoons dry sherry
¼ teaspoon freshly ground white pepper
1 egg white
1½ tablespoons cornstarch
1 tablespoon plus 3 cups peanut oil
¼ cup chicken stock
2 teaspoons potato starch, mixed with 1 tablespoon water
½ teaspoon sugar
¼ teaspoon white vinegar
4 canned water chestnuts, rinsed and halved
¼ pound snow peas (strings removed)
3 scallions, white and light green parts only, cut crosswise into ⅓-inch
pieces
1 clove garlic, finely chopped
1-inch piece ginger, peeled and thinly sliced against the grain
½ teaspoon sesame oil

To marinate the shrimp: Put shrimp, 1 tablespoon salt, and 2 cups ice-cold water into a large bowl and toss well; drain. Pour 1 cup clean ice-cold water over shrimp and repeat; drain. Pat shrimp and towel dry; return shrimp to dry bowl. Add ¼ teaspoon salt, 1 tablespoon sherry, ⅛ teaspoon pepper, and egg white; mix with your hands until evenly coated and the egg white is dispersed. Add cornstarch and 2 teaspoons peanut oil and toss well. Transfer shrimp to another bowl, discarding any marinade that clings to original bowl. Cover and refrigerate.

Mix remaining sherry, remaining salt, remaining pepper, chicken stock, potato starch, sugar, and vinegar together in a bowl. Set sauce mixture aside.

Heat 3 cups peanut oil in a wok over medium-high heat until oil reaches 300° on a deep fry thermometer. Carefully add shrimp and gently stir until shrimp turn white, about 30 seconds. Using slotted spoon, transfer shrimp to a strainer set over a medium pot. Let oil in wok reach 350°, then add water chestnuts and cook, stirring constantly, for 20 seconds. Add snow peas and cook for 2-3 seconds then quickly and carefully pour entire contents of wok (vegetables and oil) into the strainer with the shrimp, allowing oil to drain into the pot below; discard oil when cool.

Wipe out wok and heat remaining peanut oil over high heat. Add scallion, garlic, and ginger and cook, and stirring, for 10 seconds. Add reserved sauce mixture; stir constantly until it comes to a boil and thickens, 20-30 seconds. Return shrimp and vegetables to wok and toss quickly. Drizzle with sesame oil and serve immediately.

Colorful Shrimp Stir-Fry

Yields 4 servings

1 pound unpeeled large fresh shrimp
½ teaspoon salt
½ teaspoon grated orange rind
¼ teaspoon crushed red pepper
1 teaspoon light sesame oil
½ pound fresh asparagus spears
⅓ cup canned diluted chicken broth
3 tablespoons oyster sauce
1 tablespoon hoisin sauce
2 teaspoons cornstarch
3 tablespoons peanut oil
1 tablespoon minced garlic
1 tablespoon grated fresh gingerroot
1 small sweet red pepper, cut into thin strips
1 (7 ounces) jar baby corn, drained
2 teaspoons sake
Hot cooked rice

Peel and devein shrimp; rinse and pat dry. Place shrimp in a large bowl; sprinkle with salt, orange rind, and crushed red pepper. Add sesame oil, and toss gently to combine. Set aside.

Snap off tough ends of asparagus. Remove scales from stalks with a knife or vegetable peeler, if desired. Cut asparagus diagonally into 1 ½-inch pieces. Set aside.

Combine chicken broth, oyster sauce, hoisin sauce, and cornstarch in a glass measure; stir well, and set aside.

Pour peanut oil around top of preheated wok, coating sides; heat at medium high (325°) for 2 minutes. Add garlic and gingerroot, and stir-fry 30 seconds. Add shrimp mixture, and stir-fry 1 to 2 minutes or until shrimp turns pink. Remove shrimp; drain on paper towels.

Add asparagus pieces and sweet red pepper strips to wok, and stir-fry 1 minute or until vegetables are crisp-tender. Remove vegetables from wok; set aside.

Add chicken broth mixture to wok; cook, stirring gently, until mixture thickens. Add shrimp, asparagus, red pepper, baby corn, and sake, and stir-fry just until thoroughly heated. Serve over rice.

Almond-Coated Trout

Yields 6 servings

6 large trout fillets (about 3 pounds)
½ cup milk
¼ cup butter or margarine, melted
½ teaspoon almond extract
⅓ cup all-purpose flour
½ cup yellow cornmeal
½ teaspoon salt
½ teaspoon pepper
1¼ cups slivered almonds, minced
¾ cup coarsely crushed corn flakes cereal
½ cup almond, peanut, or vegetable oil
Fresh parsley sprigs (optional)

Rinse trout with cold water; pat dry, and set aside.

Combine milk, butter, and almond extract; stir well, and set aside. Combine flour and next 3 ingredients; stir well, and set aside. Combine almonds and cereal; toss gently. Dip trout in milk mixture; dredge in flour mixture. Dip again in milk mixture; coat with almond-cereal mixture.

Heat oil in a large heavy skillet. Fry trout, a few at a time, in hot oil 3 to 4 minutes on each side or until golden. Drain on paper towels. Garnish with parsley sprigs, if desired.

Note: To bake Almond-Coated Trout, omit ½ cup oil. Place coated trout fillets on a rack in a broiler pan. Bake at 500° for 4 minutes on each side or until fish flakes easily when tested with a fork.

Perfect Crab Cakes with Green Onions

1 egg beaten
2 tablespoons mayonnaise
2 tablespoons minced green onion tops
¼ teaspoon Chesapeake seasoning such as Old Bay
¼ teaspoon hot red pepper sauce
1 pound lump or backfin crabmeat, drained and picked over for shells
4 teaspoons milk
10 saltine crackers, finely crushed
6 tablespoons olive oil, for frying
Lemon wedges, for serving

Mix egg, mayonnaise, green onions, Old Bay, and hot sauce in a small bowl until mayo is completely incorporated, then set aside.

Lightly break up crabmeat in a medium bowl. Add milk; toss gently to coat. Add crushed saltines; toss gently to combine. Add egg mixture; gently toss, once again, to combine. Using a ⅓ cup measuring cup, scoop up a portion of crab, forming the mixture into a very compact cake. Repeat to make 8 cakes (can be covered with plastic wrap and refrigerated up to 8 hours ahead).

About 10 minutes before serving, heat oil in a 12-inch skillet over medium to medium-high heat. Carefully add crab cakes; sauté, turning once, until golden brown, about 3 minutes per side. Transfer to a paper towel-lined plate. Serve immediately with lemon wedges.

Crispy Fried Crab Cakes

Yields 8 to 10 servings

1 cup chopped onion
1 cup chopped celery
½ cup chopped green pepper
¼ cup melted butter or margarine
½ pound fresh crabmeat, drained and flaked
1 (8 ounce) package herb-seasoned stuffing mix
½ cup self-rising flour
3 eggs, well beaten
2 tablespoons vinegar
1 teaspoon salt
1 teaspoon dry mustard
2 to 3 teaspoons pepper
2 cups vegetable oil

Sauté onion, celery, and green pepper in butter until vegetables are tender.

Combine all ingredients except vegetable oil, stirring well. Form into patties 3 inches in diameter and ½ inch thick. Fry in hot oil (360°) until golden brown, turning once. Drain on paper towel.

Crab Cakes

Yields 6 cakes

3 white bread slices
¼ cup mayonnaise
1 large egg
1 teaspoon baking powder
1 teaspoon Old Bay seasoning
1 teaspoon Worcestershire sauce
1 teaspoon prepared mustard
¼ teaspoon salt
¼ teaspoon parsley flakes
Pinch of pepper
Dash of hot sauce
1 pound fresh jumbo lump crabmeat, drained and picked
½ cup vegetable oil

Pulse bread in food processor 6 times or until coarsely crumbled. Whisk together mayonnaise and next 9 ingredients in a large bowl; gently fold in breadcrumbs and crabmeat (being careful not to break up crab). Shape mixture into 6 patties; place on a baking sheet. Cover and chill at least 1 hour.

Cook crab cakes, in batches, in hot oil in a medium skillet over medium high heat 3 to 4 minutes on each side or until golden.

Crabmeat Imperial

Yields 4 servings

¼ cup chopped green pepper
¼ cup chopped celery
1 (2 ounce) jar diced pimiento, drained
2 tablespoons butter or margarine, melted
1 teaspoon fish seasoning
1 teaspoon butter-flavored salt
2 tablespoons chopped fresh parsley
½ teaspoon prepared mustard
Dash of hot sauce
Dash of ground red pepper
1 egg, beaten
3 tablespoons mayonnaise
1 pound fresh lump crabmeat, drained
Mayonnaise
Pimiento strips (optional)
Celery leaves (optional)
Sliced pimiento-stuffed olives (optional)

Sauté green pepper, celery, and diced pimiento in butter until tender. Add Old Bay seasoning and next 5 ingredients; stir well.

Combine egg and 3 tablespoons mayonnaise; stir in vegetable mixture. Gently stir in crabmeat. Spoon mixture into 4 lightly greased baking shells. Place shells on a baking sheet. Bake at 375° for 15 minutes. Broil 5 inches from heat for 2-3 minutes or until golden.

Top each serving with dollop of mayonnaise. If desired, garnish with pimiento strips, celery leaves, and sliced olives.

Creamed Crab Meat with Artichoke Hearts

Yields 8 servings

½ cup butter
½ cup flour
¼ cup grated onion
½ cup chopped green onion
2 tablespoons chopped parsley
2 cups whipping cream
¾ cup dry white wine
2½ teaspoons salt
½ teaspoon white pepper
¼ teaspoon cayenne pepper
2 tablespoons lemon juice
2 pounds fresh crab meat
1 (14 ounce) can artichoke hearts, drained, quartered
½ pound fresh mushrooms, thickly sliced

In a 2-quart saucepan melt butter and stir in flour. Cook 5 minutes over medium heat, stirring often. Add onions. Cook 2-3 minutes without browning. Stir in parsley. Gradually add cream and heat well. Add wine, salt, white pepper, and cayenne pepper. Blend well. Bring to a simmer, stirring occasionally. Remove from heat. When sauce has cooled to lukewarm, stir in lemon juice. In a 3-quart casserole, alternate layers of crab meat, artichoke hearts and mushrooms, spreading sauce between layers. Bake uncovered at 350° for 30-45 minutes. May be prepared in advance. Freezes well.

Herb-Crusted Orange Roughy

Yields 4 servings

¼ cup fresh orange juice
4 fillets of orange roughy or other fleshy fish
Sunflower oil or olive oil
1 tablespoon dried tarragon
1 tablespoon coarsely ground black pepper
Grated zest (rind) of two oranges

Preheat oven to 325°.
Pour orange juice into a shallow baking dish large enough to hold fish. Brush fish lightly with oil; place in baking dish.

In a bowl, combine tarragon, pepper, and grated orange zest. Sprinkle mixture on top of fish, patting it lightly to form a thin crust. Bake for 20-25 minutes, until fish flakes easily when tested with a fork.

With a long meal serving spatula, remove fish carefully to a serving dish. Fish may release a lot of liquid while cooking—this can be discarded. Serve immediately.

Scalloped Oysters

Yields 4 servings

1 pint oysters
4 tablespoons oyster liquor
2 tablespoons milk or cream
½ cup stale bread crumbs
1 cup cracker crumbs
½ cup melted butter
Salt and pepper

Mix bread and cracker crumbs and stir in butter. Put a thin layer in the bottom of a shallow, buttered baking dish, cover with half of the oysters and sprinkle with salt and pepper. Add half each, oyster liquor and milk or cream. Repeat and cover top with remaining crumbs. Bake 30 minutes in a hot oven (450°). Never allow more than two layers of oysters for scalloped oysters.

Scampi

Yields 2 to 4 servings

½ cup butter
2 tablespoons Worcestershire sauce
¼ cup sherry
1 clove garlic or a like amount of liquid garlic
2 tablespoons lemon juice
1 tablespoon sugar
1 pound raw shrimp
¼ cup parsley
Cooked rice
Parmesan cheese (optional)

In a shallow pan over low heat, melt butter. Add Worcestershire sauce, sherry, garlic, lemon juice, and sugar. Mix well, then arrange 1 pound of raw shrimp, shelled and deveined in a single layer in the pan. Spoon sauce over shrimp. Broil at low heat 8 minutes. Remove from broiler and let stand 15 minutes. Sprinkle ¼ cup minced parsley over shrimp. Broil at high heat for 3 minutes. Spoon over hot cooked rice and sprinkle with Parmesan cheese.

Garlic Shrimp

Yields 2 servings

2 dozen large fresh shrimp
¼ cup olive oil
¼ cup chopped fresh parsley
3 cloves garlic, minced
½ teaspoon dried crushed red pepper
¼ teaspoon pepper
¼ cup butter or margarine, melted
½ cup French breadcrumbs (homemade), toasted
½ cup freshly grated Parmesan cheese

Peel shrimp; devein, if desired. Arrange in a 11 x 7-inch baking dish; pour oil over shrimp. Combine parsley and next 3 ingredients; sprinkle over shrimp. Cover and bake at 300° for 15 minutes.

Turn shrimp over; drizzle with butter, and sprinkle with breadcrumbs and cheese. Bake, uncovered for 5 to 10 minutes.

Shrimp Creole

2 pounds fresh shrimp
2 cups cooked tomatoes
1 green pepper
1 medium onion
2 dashes cayenne
⅛ teaspoon black pepper
1 stalk celery
1 teaspoon salt
1 bay leaf
2 sprigs thyme
2 tablespoons butter
2 tablespoons flour

Melt butter, fry onion until wilted not brown, blend in flour, add tomatoes, minced green pepper, diced celery, thyme, bay leaf, salt, cayenne, and black pepper. Cook over low flame until slightly thick and celery and pepper are tenderized.

Drop in cooked and peeled shrimp and allow to simmer for 10 minutes. Serve on top of piles of fluffy rice.

Shrimp Amandine

Yields 4 servings

½ cup sliced (or slivered) almonds
2 tablespoons butter or margarine
¾ pound clean medium shrimp
1 can (13 ¾ ounce) chicken broth
1 (10 ounce) package frozen green peas and pearl onions
½ teaspoon dillweed
½ teaspoon salt
¼ teaspoon pepper
1½ cups dry Minute Rice
½ cup pimientos

Sauté almonds in butter until lightly browned. Add shrimp and sauté about 5 minutes until shrimp is pink. Add broth, vegetables, and seasonings. Bring to a full boil.

Stir in rice and pimentos. Cover and remove from heat. Let stand for 5 minutes. Fluff with fork.

Corn-Crisp Salmon Croquettes

1 pound can salmon, drained and flaked
½ cup Pet evaporated milk
½ cup Kellogg's Corn Flakes crumbs
¼ cup drained pickle relish
¼ cup finely cut celery
2 tablespoons finely cut onion

Mix all of the above ingredients, dip in ½ cup evaporated milk. Roll in mixture of 1 cup Kellogg's corn flake crumbs (separate from above) and 1 teaspoon Accent. Place in shallow baking pan lined with Reynolds Wrap.

Note: You can use 6 ½ ounce can of tuna, drained and flaked in place of salmon to make Tuna Croquettes.

Grilled Salmon Salad

Yields 4 servings

4 center-cut salmon fillets with skin on (about 6 ounces each)
2 tablespoons olive oil
2 tablespoons fresh lime juice
Salt and freshly ground black pepper to taste

For Salad:

4 cups arugula leaves, rinsed, well dried and coarsely chopped
2 cups pear or cherry tomatoes, halved
¼ cup diced (¼ inch) red onion
Salt and freshly ground black pepper, to taste
1 tablespoon extra-virgin olive oil
1 tablespoon red-wine vinegar

Place the salmon in a shallow dish. Combine the oil, lime juice, salt and pepper. Pour over salmon and let marinate in the refrigerator, covered, for 1 hour, turning once.

Lightly oil the grill before preheating it. Put the salmon on top and grill it, skin-side down, for 8-13 minutes (depending on thickness), until medium-rare or to desired doneness.

Meanwhile, combine all the salad ingredients in a bowl.

Place a salmon fillet in the center of each of 4 dinner plates. Divide the salad equally atop each piece of fish.

Market-Fresh Suppers

Yields 4 servings

1 (9 ounce) package refrigerated fettuccine
2 tablespoons olive oil
1 pound skinless, boneless 1-inch thick salmon, cut in 8 pieces
Salt and ground black pepper
6 cups packaged fresh baby spinach
½ cup bottled roasted red or yellow sweet peppers
½ cup reduced-calorie balsamic vinaigrette salad dressing

Prepare pasta according to package directions.

Meanwhile, brush 1 tablespoon olive oil on salmon. Sprinkle with salt and pepper. Heat an extra-large skillet over medium heat; add salmon. Cook

8 to 12 minutes or until salmon flakes, turning once. Remove salmon; cover and keep warm. Add spinach, sweet peppers, and remaining oil to skillet. Cook and stir 1 to 2 minutes, until spinach is wilted. Drain pasta; add to skillet. Add dressing; toss to coat. Season with salt and pepper. Divide spinach pasta mixture among four bowls. Top with salmon.

Poached Salmon with Horseradish Sauce

Yields 4 servings

4 cups water
1 lemon, sliced
1 carrot, sliced
1 stalk celery, sliced
1 teaspoon peppercorns
4 (4 ounce) salmon steaks
Horseradish Sauce

Combine first 5 ingredients in a large skillet; bring to a boil over medium-high heat. Cover, reduce heat, and simmer 10 minutes. Add salmon steaks; cover and simmer 10 minutes. Remove skillet from heat; let stand 8 minutes. Remove salmon steaks to serving plate; serve with Horseradish Sauce.

Horseradish Sauce

¼ cup reduced-calorie mayonnaise
¼ cup plain nonfat yogurt
2 teaspoons prepared horseradish
1 teaspoon lemon juice
½ teaspoon chopped chives

Combine all ingredients; cover and chill.

Poached Salmon

Yields 6 servings

8 garlic cloves, divided
½ cup loosely packed fresh parsley leaves
¼ cup loosely packed fresh mint leaves
½ teaspoon salt
3 tablespoons extra virgin olive oil
½ bunch fresh parsley
3 lemons, sliced
6 (6 ounce) 1-inch thick salmon fillets
Garnish with lemon slices

Process 2 garlic cloves, ½ cup parsley leaves, ¼ cup mint leaves, and ½ teaspoon salt in a food processor until smooth, stopping to scrape down sides as needed. With processor running, pour oil through food chute in a slow, steady stream, processing until smooth.

Smash remaining 6 garlic cloves, using flat side of a knife. Pour water to a depth of 2½ inches into a large skillet over medium-high heat. Add smashed garlic, ½ bunch fresh parsley, and lemon slices; bring to a boil. Add salmon fillets; return liquid to a boil, reduce heat to low, simmer 7-10 minutes or until fish flakes with a fork. Remove salmon from skillet; discard liquid in skillet. Serve salmon with garlic-parsley mixture. Garnish if desired.

Salmon on Spinach with Lemon Champagne Sauce

2 extra large eggs, separated
4 tablespoons fresh lemon juice
⅓ cup dry white champagne or prosecco (Italian sparkling wine)
2 tablespoons chopped fresh dill
Salt and pepper to taste
4 (5 ounce) salmon fillets
2 (10 ounce) bags fresh baby spinach
2 tablespoons extra virgin olive oil

In a medium bowl, beat egg whites until frothy. Whisk in yolks and lemon juice. Transfer to a small pan and slowly add champagne, stirring constantly. Turn on low heat; cook, stirring constantly, until thickened. Do not boil. Remove from heat; stir in dill, salt and pepper. Makes 1 cup.

Meanwhile, coat fleshy side of fillet with black pepper, and grill or pan-fry until done, turning once. Remove skin.

Steam spinach in a large pot or in the microwave until tender. Stir in oil.

On each of four plates, place a bed of spinach. Top with a salmon fillet. Drizzle fillet with ¼ cup sauce. Serve.

Cedar Plank-Grilled Salmon with Garlic, Lemon and Dill

Yields 8 (6 ounce) servings
1 whole fillet of salmon, about 3 pounds, skin on, scored
(up to but not through the skin)
6 tablespoons extra virgin olive oil
4 large garlic cloves, minced (generous 1 tablespoon)
¼ cup minced fresh dill
2 teaspoons salt
1 teaspoon ground black pepper
1 teaspoon lemon zest, plus lemon wedges for serving

Soak an untreated cedar plank (or planks) large enough to hold a side of the salmon (5-7 inches wide and 16-20 inches long) in water weighting it with something heavy, like a brick, so it stays submerged 30 minutes to 24 hours.

When ready to grill, either build a charcoal fire in half the grill or turn grill burners on high for 10 minutes. Meanwhile, mix oil, garlic, dill, salt, pepper, and lemon zest; rub over salmon and into scored areas to coat.

Place soaked cedar on hot grill grate, close lid and watch until wood starts to smoke, about 5 minutes. Transfer salmon to hot plank, move salmon off direct charcoal heat or turn burners to low, and cook covered until salmon is just opaque throughout (130° on a meat thermometer inserted in the thickest section) 20 to 25 minutes or longer, depending on thickness and grill temperature. Let sit 5 minutes; serve with lemon wedges.

Oven-Poached Salmon

Yields 6-8 servings

2 large carrots, diced
1 large onion, diced
¼ cup chopped flat-leaf parsley
1 salmon fillet (about 3 pounds)
½ teaspoon salt
⅛ teaspoon freshly ground black pepper
⅛ teaspoon ground allspice
½ cup white wine
½ cup water
Caper-cream or mustard sauce or sunshine pepper relish (recipes follow)
Capers and olives for garnish

Preheat oven to 350°. Combine carrot, onion, and parsley in skillet large enough to accommodate fish in one piece. Place fish on vegetables. Sprinkle with salt, pepper and allspice. Pour wine and water over fish. Bring to boil over high heat. Butter foil squares on one side and crimp over fish or cover with sheet of buttered parchment; cut vent hole in center of covering. Bake 25 minutes or until flesh is opaque at center when tested with skewer or fork. Cool fish in cooking liquid. Remove with slotted spatula and place on plate. Discard vegetables (or freeze with stock for future use in soup). Serve salmon with one or more toppings. Sprinkle capers on fish and garnish with olives.

Circular Salmon Loaf

Yields 8 servings

2 cans (about 15 ounces each) pink salmon, drained, flaked
1 (10 ounce) package frozen chopped spinach, thawed, well-drained
2½ cups shredded Jarlsberg or mild Swiss cheese, divided
1 cup fresh bread crumbs
2 eggs, lightly beaten
½ cup finely chopped onion, divided
½ cup chopped fresh parsley, divided
1 tablespoon lemon juice
¼ cup margarine
1 (18 ounce) package lemon-dill sauce mix
1 cup cold water
½ cup milk
2 cups steamed fresh vegetables, if desired

121

In a large bowl, blend salmon, spinach, 1½ cups of the cheese, bread crumbs, both eggs, ⅓ cup each onion and parsley, and the lemon juice. Mix well and spread evenly into a greased 8-inch springform pan or cake pan with removable bottom. Bake in a preheated 350° oven for 30 minutes.

Top with remaining 1 cup shredded Swiss or Jarlsberg cheese and bake 15 minutes longer. Meanwhile, in a medium saucepan, cook remaining onion and parsley in margarine until tender. Blend in sauce mix; remove from heat and gradually whisk in the water and milk. Return to medium heat; cook and stir until mixture comes to a boil. Reduce heat and simmer 1 minute, stirring often.

To serve, remove loaf from pan. Place on serving platter or low pedestal plate.

Arrange mixed cooked or steamed vegetables (broccoli and cauliflower florets, baby carrots, chopped red bell pepper) in center of loaf and serve with sauce.

Herb-Roasted Salmon with Wild Mushrooms

Yields 8 servings

8 salmon fillet pieces, skin on (about 6 ounces each)
½ pound mixed herb sprigs (parsley, thyme, rosemary, sage, marjoram, oregano), divided
2 onions, thinly sliced
1¾ cup white wine or water, divided
Salt and pepper
1 pound mixed wild or common mushrooms such as morel, cepes, chanterelle, or oyster
1 tablespoon olive oil

Preheat oven to 400°. Set salmon pieces upside down on a cutting board and slit skin with tip of sharp knife. Rinse herb sprigs and pat dry; pull off about ½ cup of the leaves and set aside for the mushrooms. Lay sliced onion and herb sprigs in the bottom of a shallow baking dish and pour 1 cup of wine over. Set salmon pieces, skin side down, over herbs and season with salt and pepper.

Bake until salmon is just opaque through the thickest part, 10-12 minutes, depending on the thickness of the fish. Meanwhile, mince reserved herbs. Put mushrooms in a colander and quickly toss under cold water. Cut off and discard any tough steams and coarsely chop mushrooms. Heat oil in a skillet; add mushrooms and sauté over medium-high heat until just tender, stirring constantly with a wooden spoon, 3 to 4 minutes.

Add remaining wine with chopped herbs, salt and pepper. Sauté over high heat, stirring 1 minute. Set aside.

When salmon is cooked, transfer to individual warmed plates. Spoon mushrooms alongside.

Boiled Live Lobster

Lobster
½ cup olive oil
Paprika
Salt

Remove claws from lobster, then split lobster in half. Crack meaty parts of claws. Put in small pan, cover with ½ cup of olive oil, sprinkle with paprika and salt. Boil for 15 minutes for 1½ pound lobster. Serve with lemon wedges and hot butter.

Lobster Thermidor

Yields 6 servings
6 large live lobsters or large frozen lobster tails
2 cloves garlic, chopped
1 onion, chopped
½ cup salt
2 teaspoons pepper
¾ cup butter, plus 3 level tablespoons butter
½ cup flour
1½ cups light cream
9 canned mushrooms, cut up
½ teaspoon Dijon mustard
3 tablespoons chopped fresh parsley
1 cup sherry
3 dashes paprika
Parmesan cheese

Put lobsters or tails to boil for 30 minutes in a pot of water seasoned with the garlic, onion, salt, and pepper. Let cool. Remove from the pot. Remove the meat from tails. Dice; set aside and reserve the shells. Melt ¾ cup butter in a pot, add the flour, and stir until smooth. Add the cream, stirring until the sauce is thick. Take off the heat and set aside. Saute the lobster meat and mushrooms in the 3 tablespoons butter for 5 minutes, then add the sherry and blend in well. Add paprika, then place the mixture in the lobster shells. Sprinkle with Parmesan cheese; put in a 450° oven and bake for 15 minutes.

Oriental Lobster Mornay

¼ teaspoon pepper
⅓ cup butter
5 tablespoons flour
1 teaspoon salt
2 cups milk
1 cup Swiss cheese
2 teaspoons soy sauce
½ cup light cream
2 cans Fancy Bean Sprout
2 cans lobster, drained
1 can (5 ounce) water chestnuts, drained and sliced
½ cup slivered green pepper
½ cup chow mein noodles

Melt butter in heavy skillet, stir in flour, salt and pepper. Gradually stir in milk. Cook over low heat, stirring constantly, until thick and smooth. Add soy sauce, cheese and cream; continue cooking slowly until cheese melts. Meanwhile, rinse bean sprouts in cold water and let drain thoroughly in colander. Add lobster, water chestnuts, green pepper, and bean sprouts to cheese sauce, blending lightly. Fill buttered 1 ½ quart casserole. Sprinkle surface with crisp noodles and dot with tablespoon of butter. Bake at 350° for 25 minutes.

Shrimp

Yields 6 servings

1 tablespoon lemon juice
1½ cups hot vegetable broth or chicken stock
1 (10 ounce) package frozen green peas, thawed
3 tablespoons cornstarch
¼ cup cold water
1 cup water chestnuts, thinly sliced
3 cups hot cooked rice

Heat oil in a deep skillet. Add uncooked shrimp and cook gently, turning them over until they turn pink. Add garlic, soy sauce, lemon juice, hot broth, or stock and green peas. Simmer until peas are just tender, three to five minutes. Stir together the cornstarch and cold water until smooth. Add with water chestnuts to shrimp mixture. Cook and stir constantly until sauce is thickened and clear. Serve over hot rice.

Shrimp Cocktail

Yields 10 servings

2 teaspoons salt
5 whole black peppercorns
2 pounds large shrimp shelled, tails intact; deveined

Cocktail Sauce

1 cup ketchup
1 tablespoon each dark-brown sugar, minced shallots and prepared horseradish
½ teaspoon grated lime zest
¼ teaspoon freshly ground black pepper
Pinch of salt
1 teaspoon fresh lime juice
8 drops hot red-pepper sauce
Ice and lime wedges

Up to 4 hours before serving: Over high heat, in large saucepan, heat 4 cups cold water, the salt and peppercorns to boiling; add shrimp. Cook 2 ½ minutes or until barely cooked; drain immediately. Place in bowl of ice and water to stop cooking and cool; drain. Cover; chill.

In bowl, mix sauce ingredients. Line platter with ice; top with shrimp and lime wedges. Serve with sauce.

Shrimp Scampi

Yields 6 servings

1 pound jumbo shrimp, butterflied
½ cup extra-virgin oil
4 large cloves garlic, minced
1 tablespoon fresh lemon juice
2 plum tomatoes, seeded, diced
2 tablespoons minced parsley
½ teaspoon dried oregano, crumbled
½ teaspoon each pepper and salt

Flatten shrimp slightly; place in bowl; add all remaining ingredients except salt. Marinate in refrigerator 2 hours, stirring shrimp once or twice.

Add salt to shrimp mixture; toss. Place shrimp on boiler pan. Place marinade in small saucepan; heat to boiling. Simmer 2 minutes or until hot. Broil shrimp 3 inches from heat source 2 minutes; turn and cook 1 minute or just until cooked through. Place on platter; pour hot marinade on top.

Easy Seafood in Sea Shells

½ cup finely chopped onions
¼ cup finely chopped green peppers
½ cup finely chopped celery
½ cup butter or oleo, melted
2 cups bread crumbs
1 cup Holmans margarine
½ cup sour cream
¼ cup white wine
¼ cup half-and-half cream or milk
1 teaspoon Worcestershire sauce
1 package cooked frozen medium shrimp (40-50 count)
1 package crab meat dried

Mix all ingredients and place in a 13x9-inch casserole dish or 12 individual shells.

Seafood Casserole with Mushrooms

Yields 14 servings

Roux:
½ cup melted butter or margarine
¼ cup flour
4 cups milk
Salt and pepper to taste
Assemble:
6 hard cooked eggs
1 pound cooked shrimp, cut into pieces
14 ounces canned tuna, drained
8 ounces canned mushrooms, drained
12 ounces crab meat
½ pound cheddar cheese, shredded
2 cups bread crumbs mixed with ½ pound melted butter

Make a roux by combining butter or margarine and flour over medium heat; stir until smooth. Add milk, slowly, stirring continually until thickened. Add in salt and pepper.

Layer next 7 ingredients in a 9x13-inch casserole dish with sauce between each layer. Bake at 325° for 45 minutes or until bubbly in center.

Seafood Casserole

Yields 6 individual casserole dishes
1 cup chopped green pepper
1½ cups chopped onion
6 ounces butter
20 shrimp, cut in pieces
1 pound crabmeat
2 lobster tails, cut in bite-size pieces
Salt and pepper to taste
½ can tomato soup
2 cans thawed cream of shrimp soup
1 cup half-and-half cream
1 cup sherry
Sprinkle of nutmeg
Buttered toast tips
Parmesan cheese

Sauté green pepper and onions in butter, then add cooked shrimp, lobster pieces and crab meat; mix in butter, green pepper and onion. Add tomato soup, cream of shrimp soup, and half-and-half. Mix well, then add sherry and nutmeg. (Do not boil). Serve over buttered toast tips, sprinkle with Parmesan cheese.

Sauce Marguery for Fish

1 tablespoon chopped parsley
3 green onions, chopped
1 clove garlic, pressed
1 rib celery, chopped
2 tablespoons butter
½ pound boiled, peeled and deveined shrimp
½ cup chopped mushrooms
3 tablespoons butter
3 tablespoons flour
1½ cups milk
1 jigger sauterne wine
¼ teaspoon grated nutmeg
Salt and pepper to taste
About 1 pound fish
1 tablespoon grated Italian cheese

Sauté parsley, onions, garlic, and celery in butter. Simmer until tender. Add cooked shrimp and mushrooms. Make a cream sauce of butter, flour, and milk, stirring constantly. Add wine, nutmeg, salt and pepper. Broil fish (use some bacon drippings on it). Place on board, and add the shrimp mushroom mixture to cream sauce; pour sauce over fish, sprinkle with cheese. We decorate board with mashed potatoes, broiled tomatoes and peas. Serve at table from board.

Herb-Roasted Chicken

Yields 6 servings

2 tablespoons butter
1 teaspoon dried sage
1 clove garlic, crushed
⅛ teaspoon black pepper
1 whole chicken (3 pounds and 5 ounces)
1 teaspoon dried rosemary
1 onion, peeled
2 cups chicken broth
6 ounces new potatoes, parboiled
3 bell peppers, deseeded and cut into quarters
2 medium zucchini, cut into chunks
1 red onion, sliced
1 tablespoon olive oil

Preheat oven to 375°. In a small bowl, combine butter, sage, garlic clove, and pepper. Carefully loosen the skin from the chicken breast, being careful not to tear it.

Spread half of the herb mixture under the skin; rub the rest on top. Sprinkle with rosemary. Place onion in chicken cavity and tie legs together with kitchen string.

Place the chicken on a rack in a roasting pan and pour broth into pan. Cover pan with foil and roast for 1 hour.

Uncover the chicken and roast until juices run clear when meat is pierced, about 40 minutes longer. Transfer to a serving dish. Let stand 15 minutes before serving.

Meanwhile, place the parboiled new potatoes, peppers, zucchini, and onion slices on a separate baking tray. Drizzle with the oil and then roast for 35-40 minutes until cooked and crisp around the edges. Arrange around chicken.

Baked Breast of Chicken

Yields 4-6 servings

6-8 ounces chicken breast halves, boned and skinned
Garlic salt
½ cup (1 stick) butter or margarine, melted
1 teaspoon paprika
3 tablespoons lemon juice
1 cup sour cream, room temperature
¼ cup sherry
2 (4 ounce) cans mushroom stems and pieces, drained
Generous dash cayenne pepper

Preheat oven to 375°. Sprinkle chicken with garlic salt to taste. Mix together melted margarine or butter, paprika, and lemon juice. Brush chicken breasts well with butter mixture and place in shallow baking pan. Bake tented with foil about 30 minutes, or until tender, brushing with remaining butter mixture occasionally to keep from drying. In a bowl, blend together sour cream, sherry, mushrooms, and cayenne pepper. Pour over chicken for last 15 minutes of baking.

Original Ranch Broiled Chicken

Yields 4 servings

1 packet (1 ounce) Hidden Valley Original Ranch Dressing Mix
2 tablespoons olive oil
1 tablespoon red wine vinegar
1 pound boneless, skinless chicken breasts and/or thighs

Combine dressing mix, oil, and vinegar in a plastic bag. Add chicken; shake, working mixture into meat. Marinate 1 hour. Broil chicken approximately 10-14 minutes total, turning once.

Chicken and Corn Pies with Cornbread Crust

1 (10 ounce) can enchilada sauce
1 (10 ounce) can Mexican diced tomatoes with lime juice and
cilantro, drained
2 cups frozen whole kernel corn
1 teaspoon chili powder
3 cups chopped cooked chicken or 2 (12.5 ounce) cans chicken drained
1 (6 ounce) package Mexican-style cornbread mix
⅔ cup milk
1 large egg
2 tablespoons vegetable oil
1 cup (4 ounces) shredded Mexican four-cheese blend, divided
Toppings:
Sliced pickled jalapeno peppers
Sour cream

Preheat oven to 375°. Stir together enchilada sauce and next 3 ingredients in a 3½-quart saucepan over medium heat until combined; cook, stirring occasionally, 10 minutes. Stir in chicken.

Whisk together cornbread mix, next 3 ingredients, and ¾ cup cheese in a small bowl just until blended.

Pour chicken mixture into 5 lightly greased (10 ounce) ramekins. Spoon cornbread mixture over hot chicken mixture. Sprinkle evenly with remaining ¼ cup cheese. Divide ramekins onto 2 jelly-roll pans. Bake at 375° for 30 minutes or until golden and bubbly. Serve with desired toppings.

Note: Mixture may be prepared in a lightly greased 11x7-inch baking dish. Bake as directed, omitting jelly-roll pans.

Baked Chicken Breasts

8 chicken breast halves, skinned and boned
8 slices Swiss cheese
1 (10¾ ounce) cream of chicken soup, undiluted
¼ cup dry white wine
1 cup herb seasoned stuffing mix, crushed
⅓ cup butter, melted

Arrange chicken in greased 13x9-inch baking dish. Top with cheese.

Mix soup and wine; spoon over chicken. Sprinkle with stuffing and drizzle melted butter over top. Bake at 350° for about 50 minutes. Sprinkle with paprika before serving.

Note: May be served with rice if desired.

Chicken in Sour Cream

3 pounds chicken, cut up
1 tablespoon flour
½ teaspoon dry mustard
1 bouillon cube
2 tablespoons Parmesan cheese
2 tablespoons sherry wine
1 teaspoon tomato paste
1 cup chicken stock
½ pint sour cream
Salt and pepper

Brown chicken in butter. Pour hot wine over chicken. Remove chicken from pan. Add paste, flour, and seasoning. Stir until smooth then add cream. Heat. Return chicken to pan and simmer 30 to 40 minutes or until chicken is tender. Serve with rice.

Cane River Chicken

Yields 12 servings

12 chicken breasts, halved, quartered, boned
1 pound medium shrimp, cooked
2 (14 ounce) cans artichoke hearts, drained
1 stick butter
2 cloves garlic, pressed
½ cup chopped celery
6 green onions, chopped
6 tablespoons flour
2 cups milk
1 cup cream
¼ cup white sauce (Sauterne)
½ teaspoon nutmeg
Salt and pepper to taste
1 tablespoon chopped parsley
½ cup Parmesan cheese (optional)

Make sauce. Cook slowly to meld flavors. Brown chicken in small amount of oil. Cover and cook until tender. At serving time, add chicken, shrimp, and artichokes. Adjust seasonings. Serve from chaffing dish into pastry shells.

Chicken and Broccoli Alfredo

Yields 4 servings

6 ounces uncooked fettuccine
1 cup fresh or frozen broccoli florets
2 tablespoons butter or margarine
1 pound skinless, boneless chicken breasts, cubed
1 can (10¾ ounce) Campbell's Condensed Cream of Mushroom Soup
½ cup milk
½ cup grated Parmesan cheese
¼ teaspoon freshly ground pepper
½ teaspoon salt

Prepare fettuccine according to package directions. Add broccoli for last 4 minutes of cooking time. Drain. In skillet over medium-high heat, heat butter. Add chicken and cook until brown, stirring often.

Add soup, milk, cheese, pepper and fettuccine mixture and cook through, stirring often.

Chicken Breasts

Yields 4 servings

1 envelope Lipton Recipe Secrets Onion Soup Mix
⅔ cup apricot or peach preserves
½ cup water
1 pound boneless skinless chicken breast halves
2 large red or green bell peppers, sliced
Hot cooked rice

In a small bowl, thoroughly combine onion soup mix, preserves and water; set aside. In aluminum foil-lined broiler pan, arrange chicken breasts; top with soup mixture. Broil 10 minutes or until chicken is done, turning once. Serve over hot rice.

Kentucky Ham

1 country ham approximately 12-15 pounds
1 bottle Coca-Cola
1 bottle ginger ale
1 apple, cubed
1 cup brown sugar
1 cup vinegar or pickle juice
2 or 3 bay leaves
2 or 3 celery stalks
Water to cover

Scrub ham with vinegar water to remove mold.

Let come to rolling boil, turn to low heat, cook 20 minutes to the pound. Turn off heat and let remain in water overnight.

Remove skin, score, stud with cloves, pineapple cherries, and brown sugar. Bake at 300° for 30 minutes.

Mandarin Ham Loaf

Yields 6 to 8 servings

2 cups bread cubes
1 pound ground cooked ham
1 pound ground beef
1 (11 ounce) can mandarin orange sections
2 eggs, beaten
½ cup seedless raisins
2 tablespoons horseradish
2 teaspoons instant minced onion
1 teaspoon tarragon
½ teaspoon salt
¼ teaspoon pepper
Horseradish sauce (recipe follows)

Combine bread cubes, ham, and beef; mix well and set aside.

Drain oranges and reserve liquid. Add reserved liquid to eggs and beat well. Stir in raisins, horseradish, and seasonings; combine with meat mixture.

Press mixture into greased 9½x5½x2 ¾-inch loaf pan; then unmold in a shallow baking pan. Bake at 350º for about 1 hour. Top with orange sections, and serve with Horseradish Sauce. Garnish as desired.

Horseradish Sauce

Yields 1¼ cups

½ cup whipping cream
¼ cup mayonnaise
2 tablespoons horseradish

Whip cream. Fold in mayonnaise and horseradish.

Ham Newburg

Yields 6 servings

1 green pepper, chopped
2 tablespoons butter or oleo, melted
2 tablespoons flour
2 tablespoons half-and-half,
1½ cups sherry
¼ cup egg yolks, beaten
3 ham, cooked and diced
2 (4 ounce) cans mushrooms, sliced and drained
Toasted triangles, toasted English muffin halves, or patty shells. (6 pieces)

Cook green pepper in butter or oleo until tender. Add flour, stirring constantly, and gradually add half-and-half. Cook, stirring constantly, until thickened. Mix in sherry. Stir a little of the hot mixture into the beaten egg yolks. Stir egg yolk mixture into remaining hot mixture. Cook, stirring constantly, until thickened. Stir in ham and mushrooms. Heat to serving temperature. Serve over choice of bread.

Breakfast Ham

Ham sliced ¼-⅓-inch thickness
Seasonings of choice
Redeye gravy (follows)

Slice ham to correct thickness. Put ham slices in a seasoned iron skillet, add just a little water and cook it real slow on medium to low heat for about 10 minutes, turning often. Remove ham slices to a warm serving platter.

Redeye Gravy

Ham drippings
1 cup water

After frying ham, pour drippings into a warm gravy bowl (do not scrape) and return skillet to hot burner. Heat skillet until remaining drippings begin to smoke and add warm water and simmer for about 1 minute. Pour in gravy bowl with drippings and serve over ham and biscuits.

Ham and Asparagus Strata

Yields 6 servings

4 English muffins, torn or cut into bite-size pieces (4 cups)
2 cups cubed cooked ham (10 ounces)
2 cups cut-up fresh cooked asparagus or broccoli
4 ounces shredded Swiss cheese
4 eggs, beaten
¼ cup dairy sour cream
1¼ cups milk
2 tablespoons finely chopped onion
1 tablespoons Dijon-style mustard
⅛ teaspoon black pepper

In greased 2 quart square baking dish, spread half the muffin pieces. Top with ham, asparagus, and cheese. Top with remaining muffin pieces.

In bowl whisk together eggs and sour cream. Stir in milk, onion, mustard, and ⅛ teaspoon black pepper. Pour over layers in dish. Cover; chill for 2 to 24 hours.

Bake, uncovered in 325° oven for 60-65 minutes or until internal temperature registers 170° on an instant-read thermometer. Let stand 10 minutes before serving.

Spanish Bacon

6 thick slices pepper bacon
½ cup milk
½ cup flour
Oil for browning

Dip bacon slices in milk, then flour. Place in a heavy skillet that has a little oil in it. Cook until brown and crispy. Drain on paper towels.

Note: This is good served with summer vegetables and makes a good bacon and tomato sandwich. It does not shrink!

Grilled Stuffed Franks

Yields 8 servings

1 (8 ounce) can tomato sauce
1 tablespoon sugar
2 tablespoons spicy brown mustard
½ teaspoon garlic powder
8 frankfurters
6 small green onions, chopped
8 slices bacon
8 hot dog buns

Combine tomato sauce, sugar, mustard, and garlic powder; stir well. Slice frankfurters lengthwise to make a pocket. Brush inside each pocket with sauce; sprinkle with onion. Wrap each frankfurter with bacon, securing with a wooden toothpick.

Cook frankfurters for 10 to 15 minutes or until bacon is crispy, turning often and basting with remaining sauce. Serve in hot dog buns.

Delicious Frankfurters

8 frankfurters
8 tablespoons shredded cheddar cheese
Mustard
8 hot dog buns
8 slices of bacon

Make a pocket in each frank. Pour mustard in bottom, and cheese on top. Wrap each with a slice of bacon. Hold with half of a wooden toothpick.

Line broiler pan with foil. Broil franks, turning until bacon is crisp and down. Serve in toasted bun.

Savannah Pork Chops and Rice

Yields 4 servings

4 (¾-inch-thick) boneless pork loin chops
2 tablespoons vegetable oil
¼ cup diced onion
1 celery rib, sliced
2 (8 ounce) cans tomato sauce
1 cup uncooked long-grain rice
1½ cups water
2 tablespoons brown sugar
1 teaspoon salt
½ teaspoon dried basil

Cook pork chops in hot oil in a large skillet over medium-high heat for 4 minutes on each side or until browned. Remove pork from skillet.

Sauté onion and celery in skillet over medium-high heat for 2 minutes. Drain, if necessary. Stir in tomato sauce and next 5 ingredients; top with pork, and bring to a boil. Cover, reduce heat, and simmer mixture for 25 minutes.

Stuffed Pork Chops

Dressing
1 cup cornbread crumbs
½ cup milk
½ teaspoon salt
2 tablespoons minced parsley or dried parsley
1 small onion chopped
1 cup bread crumbs
1 egg
Dash of pepper

Season pocket of pork chops lightly with salt and pepper. Moisten cornbread and bread crumbs with milk, beaten egg, salt, and seasonings. Stuff pork chops with dressing and skewer with toothpicks. Flour stuffed pork chops on both sides. Brown in oil at low temperature to get an even color. Top with raw onion ring. Transfer to baking dish and add a small amount of water. Cover and bake at 350° for 1 hour. Uncover and bake 15 minutes longer.

Note: Have your butcher cut pork chops, rib or loin, at least one inch thick. Ask them to put a pocket in each chop to hold the dressing. Also chops may be prepared and placed in baking dish and baked later in the day.

Peachy Pork Chops

Yields 4 servings

4 (1-inch-thick) pork chops
¼ teaspoon seasoned salt
¼ teaspoon onion powder
1 (16 ounce) can sliced peaches, undrained
2 tablespoons brown sugar
¼ teaspoon dried whole basil
2 tablespoons butter or margarine

Place pork chops on a lightly greased rack of broiler pan. Sprinkle with seasoned salt and onion powder. Broil 4 inches from heat for approximately 7 minutes on each side.

Combine peaches and remaining ingredients in a small saucepan, stirring well. Cook, uncovered, over low heat 10 minutes, stirring often. Arrange chops on a platter. Pour sauce over chops.

Pork Chop Delight

Yields 2 servings

½ cup uncooked wild rice
3 cups water, divided
1 teaspoon salt
2 tablespoons chopped fresh parsley
1 (1⅜ ounce) package onion soup mix
2 (1½-inch-thick) loin pork chops
Salad oil
Pepper to taste

Combine rice, 2 cups cold water, and salt; bring to a boil. Simmer 40 minutes or until rice is tender. Add parsley and almonds, stirring to mix. Set aside.

Bring 1 cup water to a boil; add onion soup mix. Set aside.

Cut deep pockets in chops. Brown in hot salad oil; cool. Stuff with rice mixture, and place in a 2-quart casserole. Pour onion soup mixture over chops and sprinkle with pepper. Cover and bake at 350° for 1 hour or until pork chops are tender.

Baked San Francisco Chops

Yields 4 servings

4 pork chops (½ to ¾-inch thick, about 1½ pounds)
1 tablespoon oil
1 clove garlic, minced

Sauce:
2 teaspoons oil
4 tablespoons dry sherry or broth
4 tablespoons soy sauce
2 tablespoons brown sugar
¼ teaspoon crushed red pepper
2 teaspoons cornstarch
2 tablespoons water

Trim pork chops of fat. Heat oil in skillet. Brown chops on both sides. Remove and add a little more oil if needed.

Sauté garlic for a minute, being careful not to burn it. Combine oil, sherry or broth, soy sauce, brown sugar, and red pepper.

Place chops in skillet. Pour sauce over them. Cover tightly. Simmer over low heat until chops are tender and cooked through, about 30-35 minutes. Add a little water, 1 to 2 tablespoons if needed to keep sauce from cooking down too much. Turn once.

Remove chops to platter. Dissolve cornstarch in water. Cook until thickened. Pour over chops and serve.

Note: This recipe is good served with thin spaghetti or noodles tossed with butter and sauce, green salad with sliced cucumber and dinner rolls. For dessert, butter cookies and fresh pineapple. Boneless pork loin chops can be used. Trim fat and pound to ¼-inch thickness. Cooking takes only 20 minutes.

Microwave San Francisco Chops

Yields 4 servings

4 pork chops, ½-¾-inch thick, boneless
1 tablespoon oil
1 clove garlic, minced
3 tablespoons dry sherry or broth
3 tablespoons soy sauce
1½ tablespoons brown sugar
¼ teaspoon crushed red pepper
1½ teaspoons cornstarch
1½ tablespoons water

Trim pork chops of excess fat. Then in a microwaveable shallow dish, combine the oil and garlic. Spread evenly in dish. Microwave at high power for 1 minute.

Combine sherry, soy sauce, brown sugar, and pepper in bowl. Add pork chops to dish, turning over in garlic oil.

Pour sauce mixture over chops. Cover with wax paper. Microwave at high power for 4 minutes, turning chops and dish once after 2 minutes.

Keep covered. Microwave at medium power for 12-15 minutes or until meat is tender and no pink remains. Remove chops to serving dish.

Dissolve cornstarch in water. Stir into pan juices. Microwave at high power for 1 to 2 minutes until thickened. Leave uncovered and stir once.

Pour sauce over chops and serve.

Note: For microwaving, the rounder the shape of the container, the better. Oval dishes and oblong dishes with rounded corners are good shapes. Microwave energy is attracted to the square corners and food overcooks in those areas.

Southern Pork Chops

Yields 6 servings

6 center-cut loin pork chops, cut 1¼-inch thick
3 cups cooked flaky dry rice
6 large slices onion, cut ¼-inch thick
6 large green pepper slices, cut 1-inch thick
6 large slices tomato, cut ¼-inch thick
Salt

On a grill or frying pan, brown pork chops on both sides for 10 minutes on high heat. Place chops in a 3-inch deep baking pan. Cover each chop with onion slice, then a tomato slice, sprinkle well with salt. Put cleaned pepper ring around onion and tomato slice, stuff pepper ring with cooked rice. Pour 2 cups water into pan, cover with aluminum foil. Bake in 300° oven for 3 ½ hours. Baste every 1½ hours with pan drippings, covering rice well.

Crown Roast Pork with Fresh Sage

10 to 12 chops from the rib end of a pork loin
Freshly ground black pepper
Salt
Fresh sage leaf
Fresh sage and bread dressing (recipe follows)

Have the butcher make a crown of at least 10-12 chops from the rib end of a pork loin (fewer chops will not form the crown). If more servings are needed, the rib ends of two loins may be tied together to make a spectacular crown roast.

Rub the meat with freshly ground black pepper and salt to taste. Tuck a small piece of fresh sage leaf in between each rib. Place the prepared sage dressing in center of the crown. Cut a circle of heavy aluminum foil to make a cape to cover the ends of the rib bones and the dressing, closing it down tightly to keep the bones from charring, but leaving the bottom portion of the roast uncovered. Insert the thermometer between the ribs, not touching the foil. Place the roast on a rack in the roasting pan and roast the crown uncovered in a 325° oven allowing 35 minutes per pound, or until a meat thermometer registers the internal temperature to be 170°.

Baste the outside of the roast during the last hour with the drippings from the pan, but do not baste the stuffing.

Transfer roast and stuffing to a hot platter. Garnish the bone ends with paper frills, pickled crab apples, or soft, uncooked pitted prunes.

Fresh Sage and Bread Dressing

Yields 4 servings of dressing
4 cups firm white bread pieces, such as Pepperidge Farm
½ cup finely chopped celery and celery leaves
¼ cup chopped onion
¼ teaspoon salt
¼ teaspoon pepper
1 tablespoon finely snipped fresh sage leaves
1 egg, beaten, plus water to make ⅔ cup liquid
¼ cup melted butter

Place the bread slices in a large bowl, add the celery, onion, salt, pepper, and sage. Toss to mix. Beat the egg in a measuring cup with a fork, then add water to make ⅔ cup liquid. Scatter the egg-water mixture over the dressing a little at a time, tossing it all the while with a fork to moisten the bread evenly. Add the melted butter and toss again. Place the stuffing in the top of pork and bake as directed in the Crown Roast recipe above.

Note: For extra dressing double, triple, or quadruple the above recipe and bake amount not needed to stuff the crown of the roast in a loaf pan or casserole of appropriate size for 30 to 45 minutes, until top is browned and dressing firm, at a temperature of 325° to 350°.

Pork Tenderloin with Orange Marmalade

Yields 4 servings
1½ tablespoons coarse mustard
1 clove garlic, minced
¼ teaspoon dried whole rosemary
¼ teaspoon pepper
1 pound pork tenderloin
¼ cup low-sugar orange marmalade, divided
Vegetable cooking spray
½ cup water
¼ cup ready-to-serve, no-salt-added chicken broth

Combine first 4 ingredients; set aside. Trim fat from tenderloin. Slice tenderloin lengthwise, cutting almost to, but not through, outer edge. Spread mustard mixture in pocket; press gently to close. Tie tenderloin securely with heavy string at 2-inch intervals. Spread 2 tablespoons orange marmalade over tenderloin. Place tenderloin on rack coated with cooking spray. Place rack in broiler pan; add water to pan. Bake at 325° for 40-45 minutes or until meat thermometer inserted into thickest portion registers 160°.

Cook remaining 2 tablespoons orange marmalade and chicken broth 2 to 3 minutes or until thickened. Slice tenderloin; spoon sauce over slices, and serve.

Hong Kong Pork Chops

Yields 2 serves

2 loins or rib pork chops, 1-inch thick
1 tablespoon oyster sauce
1 tablespoon soy sauce
⅓ cup bread crumbs
⅛ teaspoon garlic salt
¼ teaspoon ground ginger
2 tablespoons dry onion soup mix

Combine oyster sauce and soy sauce in shallow bowl or pie plate. Combine crumbs, garlic powder, ginger, and onion soup mix on waxed paper. Dip chops in sauce mixture, then in crumbs and in the sauce and crumbs again to double-coat them. Place meaty side toward outside of dish, on a cooking rack set in a 12x8-inch microwave-proof baking dish. Cover with paper towel. Microwave 16-18 minutes per pound, rearranging chops once during the cooking.

Note: If desired, use 4 (½-inch thick) chops, coating once.

Pork Chops with Vegetables

Yields 8 servings

3 tablespoons vegetable oil
8 lean pork chops
1 (15 ounce) can stewed tomatoes
¾ cups water
1 cup minced celery
1 large minced green pepper
1 medium minced onion
1 bay leaf
1 thyme sprig
¼ teaspoon paprika
Salt and pepper to taste

Heat oil in a large deep skillet. Add chops and brown on both sides.

Turn stewed tomatoes into a bowl. Add water, celery, green peppers, onion, bay leaf, thyme, paprika, salt and pepper and mix well.

Remove excess fat from skillet; add tomato mixture. Cover and bake at 350° for about 2 hours or until tender. Serve pork chops with pilaf or potatoes. Pass gravy separately.

Roast Pork Loin with Orange Juice

Yields 4 servings

¾ cup orange juice
¾ teaspoon paprika
¾ teaspoons garlic powder
½ teaspoon onion powder
½ teaspoon dried oregano
½ teaspoon salt
½ teaspoon ground black pepper
1 center-cut loin of pork on the bone
¾ cup white wine or nonalcoholic white wine

Preheat oven to 450°. In a small bowl, combine paprika, garlic powder, onion powder, oregano, salt, and pepper. Pat mixture over top of pork and place pork in a small, heavy roasting pan or heavy oven-safe skillet.

Roast 10 minutes. Reduce heat to 325° and pour orange juice and wine around (not over) the pork. Roast until the pan juices run clear and a meat thermometer registers 160° for medium, 1 to 1 ¼ hours.

Remove pork from oven and allow to rest 15 minutes in pan. There should be about ⅓ cup juice left in the pan. If more juice remains, remove pork to the platter and cook over medium-low heat until juices are reduced to ⅓ cup. Thinly slice pork and spoon pan juices over the top.

Glorified Pork Chops

Yields 6 servings

1 tablespoon vegetable oil
6 pork chops, each cut ½-inch thickness (about 1 ½ pounds)
1 medium onion, sliced
1 (10¾ ounce) can Campbell's Cream of Mushroom Soup
¼ cup water

In a skillet over medium heat, in a hot oil, cook chops ½ at a time with onion 10 minutes or until browned on both sides. Spoon off fat.

Stir in soup and water. Reduce heat to low. Cover; simmer for 10 minutes, or until chops are fork-tender, stirring occasionally.

Glazed Country Ribs

Yields 4 servings

2 pounds country-style pork ribs
1¾ teaspoons salt, divided
¼ teaspoon ground black pepper, divided
¾ cup orange juice
2 tablespoons lemon juice
½ cup firmly packed brown sugar
1 bay leaf
1½ teaspoons garlic powder
1 teaspoon lemon peel
¾ teaspoon ground ginger
¼ teaspoon ground cloves

Preheat oven to 400°. Cut ribs into single rib portions. Sprinkle both sides with ¾ teaspoon of the salt and ⅛ teaspoon of black pepper.

Place ribs on a rack in a foil-lined shallow open roasting pan. Bake for 30 minutes. Reduce heat to 350°. Turn ribs and bake for 20 minutes longer. Pour off fat.

Meanwhile, prepare sauce by combining in a medium saucepan orange and lemon juices, brown sugar, bay leaf, garlic powder, lemon peel, ginger, cloves and remaining 1 teaspoon salt and ⅛ teaspoon black pepper. Bring to boil.

Reduce heat and simmer, uncovered, until mixture is reduced to ½ cup, about 15 minutes. Brush on pork ribs. Return to oven for 10 minutes, turn and brush with sauce. Bake until glazed, about 10 minutes longer.

Glazed Pork Tenderloin

Yields 6 to 8 servings

2 tablespoons Dijon mustard
½ teaspoon minced garlic
½ teaspoon dried rosemary leaves
½ teaspoon dried thyme leaves
¼ teaspoon pepper
2 tablespoons honey
2 (1 pound) pork tenderloins, trimmed of fat

Preheat oven to 325°. In a small bowl, mix together mustard, garlic, rosemary, thyme, pepper, honey. Coat tenderloins with mixture.

Place tenderloins on nonstick baking sheet coated with nonstick cooking spray or on rack in shallow roasting pan. Bake 40-45 minutes or until meat thermometer inserted into thickest portion registers 160°. Slice tenderloins and serve.

Lamb Chops with Orange Mint Sauce

3 tablespoons butter or margarine
4 lamb shoulder chops, well trimmed
2 tablespoons water
1 teaspoon cider vinegar
1 teaspoon salt
⅛ teaspoon pepper
Orange Mint Sauce (recipe sauce follows)
Mint leaves or orange slices for garnish

In a large skillet, over medium heat, melt butter. Add chops and brown about 5 minutes on each side. Meanwhile, in a small bowl, combine water, vinegar, salt and pepper; mix well. When chops are browned, add mixture to skillet. Cover, reduce heat and simmer 20 minutes longer or until lamb is fork-tender. Place on heated serving platter. Serve with Orange Mint Sauce. Garnish with mint leaves or orange slices, if desired.

Orange Mint Sauce

1 tablespoon grated orange peel
½ cup orange juice
¼ cup cider vinegar
2 tablespoons sugar
1½ teaspoons dried mint flakes or ¼ cup finely chopped mint leaves
¼ teaspoon ground ginger
1 tablespoon water
1 teaspoon corn starch

In a small saucepan, over medium heat, combine orange peel, orange juice, vinegar, sugar, mint and ginger. Cook, stirring occasionally, about 2 minutes or until mixture boils. In cup, combine water and corn starch, mixing well. Stir into boiling sauce, boil 1 minute, stirring constantly.

Turkey and Dressing Roll Ups

Yields 6 servings
6 slices deli roasted turkey breast sliced ⅛-inch thick
4 cups your favorite dressing
1 cup chicken broth
Curry Sauce

Place about 2 tablespoons dressing across one of the turkey slices and roll up. Place in a 8x8 Pyrex dish with seam side down. Repeat with other slices of turkey and dressing. Pour broth over all. Bake in conventional oven 25-30 minutes at 350° covered with foil or bake in microwave covered with plastic for about 6 minutes on medium heat.

I like to serve them with Curry Sauce.

Note: This makes a nice Sunday dinner. The rolls may be made ahead, sauced, and refrigerated.

Curry Sauce

2 tablespoons butter
2 tablespoons flour
½ teaspoon salt
1 teaspoon curry powder
1 cup of milk

In a small microwaveable bowl melt the butter ½ a minute at medium temperature. Stir in flour, salt, and curry powder. Slowly add the milk and stir. Microwave about 6 minutes, stirring half way through cooking.

At serving time, I spoon Curry Sauce over the center of turkey roll.

Note: The sauce may be made ahead of time and heated at serving time.

Turkey Roll Ups with Herb Stuffing

4 cups of Pepperidge Farm herb stuffing
2 eggs or one extra large
½ teaspoon fresh ground pepper
½ teaspoon dry basil
1½ cups chicken broth, heated
8 slices deli baked turkey at ⅛-inch thick
Curry Sauce

Mix first five ingredients for the stuffing.

Lay turkey slices out flat; put 2 thick tablespoons of stuffing on one end and roll up. Hold with ½ toothpick. Repeat with rest of turkey. Place in a baking dish and drizzle a small amount of broth over all. Cover and refrigerate overnight. An hour before serving time, bring to room temperature and bake about 30 minutes at 325° covered. Serve with Curry Sauce. Pour sauce over the turkey rolls after removing the toothpicks. Sprinkle with paprika.

Note: You may make sauce with mushroom soup or celery soup undiluted and add small amount of broth and curry. Heat slowly.

Creamy Ham-Chicken Medley

Yields 12 servings

1 tablespoon butter or margarine
½ cup sliced fresh mushrooms
⅓ cup butter or margarine
⅓ cup all-purpose flour
2½ to 3 cups milk, divided
1 cup whipping cream
1 cup freshly grated Parmesan cheese
½ teaspoon salt
¼ teaspoon freshly ground nutmeg
Dash of ground red peppers
2 cups chopped cooked chicken
2 cups chopped cooked ham
2 (10 ounce) packages frozen puff pastry shells, baked
Paprika

Melt 1 tablespoon butter in a large saucepan over medium heat; add mushrooms, and cook until tender, stirring constantly. Remove from saucepan; set aside.

Melt ⅓ cup butter in saucepan over low heat; add flour, stirring until smooth. Cook 1 minute, stirring constantly. Gradually add 2½ cups milk; cook over medium heat, stirring constantly, until thickened and bubbly. Stir in whipping cream and next 5 ingredients. Cook, stirring constantly, until cheese melts and mixture is smooth; stir in chicken and ham. Add enough of remaining ½ cup milk for thinner consistency, if desired. To serve, spoon into shells and sprinkle with paprika.

Note: Creamy Ham-Chicken Medley may be served over hot cooked angel hair pasta instead of pastry. Sprinkle with freshly grated Parmesan cheese, if desired.

Swiss Chicken Casserole

Yields 6 servings

6 chicken breast halves, skinned and boned
6 (4x4 inch) slices Swiss cheese
1 (10¾ ounce) can cream of chicken soup, undiluted
¼ cup milk
2 cups herb-seasoned stuffing mix
¼ cup butter or margarine, melted

Arrange chicken breasts in a lightly greased 12 x 8 x 2-inch baking dish. Top with cheese slices.

Combine soup and milk; stir well. Spoon sauce over chicken; sprinkle with stuffing mix. Drizzle butter over crumbs; cover and bake at 350° for 50 minutes. To freeze, prepare and cover tightly and freeze. To defrost, thaw casserole in refrigerator; cover and reheat at 350° for 45 minutes or until heated well.

Chicken and Artichokes

Yields 4 servings

4 bone-in chicken breast halves
9 tablespoons butter or margarine, divided
1 cup sliced fresh mushrooms
½ small onion, diced
1 garlic clove, minced
¼ cup dry white wine
¼ cup all-purpose flour
1½ cups milk
2 (14 ounce) cans artichoke heart quarters, drained and chopped
¼ cup grated Parmesan cheese
½ teaspoon salt
¼ teaspoon pepper
1 teaspoon chopped fresh parsley

Remove and discard skin and bones from chicken breasts. Cut chicken breasts into strips, and set aside. Melt 3 tablespoons butter in a large nonstick skillet over medium heat; add mushrooms and onion, and sauté 6 minutes. Add garlic, and sauté 2 minutes. Remove mushroom mixture from skillet.

Melt 2 tablespoons butter in the same skillet over medium heat; add chicken strips, and cook 10 minutes or until chicken is tender. Stir in wine, and cook 5 minutes. Return mushroom mixture to skillet, stirring well. Remove skillet from heat. Melt remaining 4 tablespoons butter in a small saucepan. Whisk in flour until blended and smooth. Gradually whisk in milk, and cook, whisking constantly, 5 minutes or until mixture thickens. Stir in artichokes and next 3 ingredients.

Spoon chicken mixture into an 11 x 7-inch baking dish; top evenly with artichoke mixture. Bake at 300° for 15 minutes or until bubbly. Sprinkle with parsley.

Note: Chicken broth may be substituted for white wine.

Hot Chicken Supreme

Yields 6-8 servings

3 whole chicken breasts, cooked and diced
1½ cups chopped celery
1 cup shredded cheddar cheese
1 cup mayonnaise
¼ cup milk
¼ cup slivered almonds, toasted
¼ cup chopped pimiento
2 tablespoons dry sherry
2 teaspoons chopped onion
½ teaspoon poultry seasoning
½ teaspoon grated lemon rind
1 (3 ounce) can Chinese noodles

Combine all ingredients except noodles; stir well. Spoon chicken mixture into a greased 1½-quart casserole, and top with noodles. Bake at 350° for 30 minutes.

Hearty Tex-Mex Squash Chicken Casserole

Yields 6-8 servings

1 (10 ounce) package frozen chopped spinach, thawed
3 medium-size yellow squash, thinly sliced
1 large red or green bell pepper, cut into ½-inch pieces
1 small yellow onion, thinly sliced
2 tablespoons peanut oil
3 cups shredded cooked chicken or turkey
12 (6 inch) corn tortillas, cut into 1-inch pieces
1 (10¾ ounce) can cream of celery soup, undiluted
1 (8 ounce) container sour cream
1 (8 ounce) jar picante sauce
1 (4.5 ounce) can chopped green chiles, undrained
1 (1.4 ounce) envelope fajita seasoning
2 cups (8 ounce) shredded sharp cheddar cheese, divided

Drain spinach well, pressing between paper towels; set aside. Sauté squash, bell pepper, and onion in hot oil in a large skillet over medium high heat 6 minutes or until tender. Remove from heat.

Stir in spinach, chicken, next 6 ingredients, and 1 ½ cups cheese. Spoon into a lightly greased 13x9-inch baking dish. Bake at 350° for 30 minutes. Sprinkle with remaining ½ cup cheese, and bake 5 more minutes.

Golden Chicken and Rice Squares

Yields 6 servings

2 tablespoons minced onion
¼ cup butter or margarine
⅓ cup flour
1 teaspoon salt
⅛ teaspoon ground black pepper
¼ teaspoon poultry seasoning
1¼ cups chicken broth
½ cup milk
2 cups chopped cooked chicken
2 cups cooked rice
¼ cup each chopped green pepper and pimientos
2 eggs, slightly beaten
⅔ cup buttered cereal crumbs
Mushroom Sauce (optional)

Cook onion in butter until soft. Stir in flour, seasonings, broth, and milk. Cook, stirring, until thickened and smooth. Combine chicken, rice, vegetables, and eggs. Stir in sauce. Pour into a buttered 10x6x2-inch baking dish. Sprinkle top with crumbs. Bake at 350° about 30 minutes, or until set. Cut into squares to serve. Serve with Mushroom Sauce.

Mushroom Sauce

1 (10¾ ounce) can condensed cream of mushroom soup
¼ cup milk
1 can (2 ounces) sliced mushrooms

To prepare mushroom sauce, combine 1 can (10¾ ounces) condensed cream of mushroom soup, ¼ cup milk, and 1 can (2 ounces) sliced mushrooms. Heat through.

Southwestern Chicken and Taco Casserole

Yields 4 servings

1 can (35 ounce) whole tomatoes
1 cup chopped onion
1 tablespoon vegetable oil
2 cloves garlic, crushed
1 can (8 ounce) tomato sauce
1 (4 ounce) jar pimientos, drained and sliced
1 to 3 teaspoons finely chopped pickled jalapeno peppers (optional)
3 tablespoons fresh coriander or 3 tablespoons chopped parsley
½ teaspoon ground coriander
1 teaspoon ground cumin
⅛ teaspoon black pepper
1 pound boneless, skinned chicken breasts
1 box (4½ ounce) taco shells
6 ounces Monterey Jack or cheddar cheese, shredded (1½ cups)

Drain tomatoes, reserving ½ cup liquid. Chop tomatoes and reserve. Sauté onion in oil in large skillet until softened, 3 minutes. Add garlic; sauté 1 minute. Stir in chopped tomatoes and liquid, tomato sauce, pimiento, jalapeno pepper, if using, coriander, cumin, and pepper. Bring to boiling; lower heat and simmer 10 to 15 minutes.

Preheat oven to moderate 350°. Cut chicken crosswise into thin strips. Add to skillet. Cook 5 minutes or until chicken is cooked through. Reserve.

Crush taco shells into small pieces. Sprinkle ⅔ into 11¾x7½x1½-inch baking dish. Spoon in chicken mixture; sprinkle with shells. Top with cheese.

Bake in preheated moderate oven for 30 to 35 minutes or until bubbly.

To freeze: Prepare casserole but do not cook. Seal tightly with plastic wrap or aluminum foil, label, date, and freeze. Thaw later in refrigerator for 12-24 hours. Loosely cover with foil and bake in preheated 350° oven for 30 minutes. Remove foil and bake 15 minutes or until bubbly or lightly browned.

Crunchy Turkey Casserole

Yields 6 servings

3 cups chopped cooked turkey
1 cup chopped celery
¼ cup chopped onion
2 (10¾ ounce) cans cream of mushroom soup, undiluted
1 (8 ounce) can sliced water chestnuts, drained
2 (2 ounce) jar diced pimiento, drained
1 (2 ounce) package slivered almonds
½ cup Chinese noodles

Combine all ingredients except noodles; spoon mixture into a lightly greased 12x8x2-inch baking dish. Cover with heavy-duty plastic wrap; fold back a small corner of wrap to allow steam to escape. Microwave at high 12-15 minutes or until thoroughly heated, stirring after 6 minutes. Sprinkle with Chinese noodles and serve immediately.

Chicken and Wild Rice Casserole

2 (6.2 ounce) packages fast-cooking long-grain and wild rice mix
¼ cup butter or margarine
2 medium onions, chopped
4 celery ribs, chopped
2 (8 ounce) cans sliced water chestnuts, drained
5 cups chopped cooked chicken
4 cups (16 ounces) shredded cheddar cheese, divided
1 (10¾ ounce) cans cream of mushroom soup, undiluted
1 (16 ounce) container sour cream
1 cup milk
½ teaspoon salt
½ teaspoon pepper
½ cup soft bread crumbs

Prepare rice mix according to package directions; set aside. Melt butter in a large skillet over medium heat; add onion, celery, and water chestnuts. Sauté 10 minutes or until tender. Stir in rice, chicken, 3 cups cheese, soup, and next 4 ingredients. Spoon mixture into lightly greased 15x10-inch baking dish or a 4-quart casserole. Top casserole evenly with bread crumbs. Bake at 350° for 30 minutes. Sprinkle with remaining 1 cup cheese; bake 5 more minutes.

In order to make ahead, freeze unbaked casserole up to 1 month, if desired (do not sprinkle with cheese before freezing). Let stand at room temperature 1 hour. Bake, covered at 350° for 30 minutes. Uncover casserole, and bake 55 more minutes. Sprinkle with 1 cup cheese, and bake 5 more minutes.

Note: Casserole may also be baked at 350° in two 11x7-inch dishes for 25 minutes. Sprinkle with ½ cup cheese and bake 5 more minutes.

Chicken Breasts with Crabmeat Stuffing

Yields 12 servings

12 chicken breast halves, skinned and boned
½ cup finely chopped onion
½ cup finely chopped celery
¼ cup finely chopped green pepper
¼ cup butter or margarine
½ pound lump crabmeat
2 cups seasoned stuffing mix
1 egg, beaten
¼ cup teaspoon pepper
¼ teaspoon garlic salt
¼ teaspoon Creole seasoning
¾ cup butter or margarine
2 cups corn flake crumbs
1 (⅞ ounce) envelope béarnaise sauce (optional)

Place chicken breast halves on sheet of waxed paper. Flatten chicken to ¼-inch thickness using a meat mallet or rolling pin.

Sauté onion, celery, and green pepper in ¼ cup melted butter in a large skillet. Remove from heat. Add next 6 ingredients and ¼ cup butter; mix well.

Spread about ¼ cup crabmeat mixture on each chicken breast; roll up jellyroll fashion, pressing edges to seal. Cover and refrigerate 30 minutes.

Dip each chicken roll in remaining ½ cup melted butter, and dredge in corn flake crumbs. Place seam side down in a greased 13x9x2-inch baking dish. Cover and bake at 350° for 45 minute. Uncover and bake an additional

10 minutes or until golden brown. Prepare béarnaise sauce according to the package directions, and serve over chicken rolls, if desired.

Chicken Casserole

¼ cup salad oil
1 can Campbell's onion soup, French or cream style
1 cup water
1 cup raw rice, either brown or white
4-6 chicken breasts, skinned, and if desired boned
Season to taste

Mix in a pot ¼ cup salad oil, 1 can of Campbell's onion soup, 1 cup water, and bring ingredients to a boil. Add 1 cup regular raw rice, either brown or white. Pour into a shallow casserole.

Put 4 to 6 chicken breasts, skinned, and if desired boned, on top of rice. Season to taste. Bake, covered at 325° for 1 hour or until rice is done.

Hot and Cheesy Chicken Casserole

Yields 8 to 10 servings
3 cups chopped cooked chicken
1 (14 ounce) package frozen broccoli florets
2 cups cooked rice
1½ cups frozen peas
1 (10.75 ounce) can condensed cream of chicken soup
1 (10.75 ounce) can condensed fiesta nacho cheese soup
1 (10 to 10.5 ounce) can diced tomatoes and green chilies
½ cup milk
½ teaspoon crushed red pepper (optional)
½ cup shredded cheddar cheese (2 ounces)
½ cup shredded mozzarella cheese (2 ounces)
1 cup crushed rich round crackers

Preheat oven to 350°. Place chicken in bottom of 3-quart rectangular baking dish. In large bowl combine broccoli, rice, and peas. Spread mixture over the chicken. In medium bowl combine cream of chicken soup, nacho cheese soup, diced tomatoes, milk, and crushed red pepper. Stir in ¼ cup of the mozzarella cheese. Pour mixture over broccoli mixture in baking dish. Sprinkle crushed crackers evenly over all. Top with remaining cheddar and mozzarella cheeses.

Bake, uncovered, 35-40 minutes or until topping is golden.

Note: If you do not have leftover rice, cook ⅔ cup long-grain white rice or brown rice in 1 ⅓ cup boiling water for 15 minutes (40 minutes for brown rice) or until water is absorbed.

Chicken Florentine Artichoke Bake

Yields 6-8 servings

8 ounce dried bow tie pasta
1 small onion, chopped
1 tablespoon butter
2 eggs
1¼ cups milk
1 teaspoon dried Italian seasoning
¼ to ½ teaspoon crushed red pepper (optional)
2 cups chopped cooked chicken
2 cups shredded Monterey Jack cheese
1 (14 ounce) can artichoke hearts, drained and quartered
1 (10 ounce) package frozen chopped spinach, thawed and well drained
½ cup oil-packed dried tomatoes, drained and chopped
¼ cup grated Parmesan cheese
½ cup soft bread crumbs
½ teaspoon paprika
1 tablespoon butter, melted

Preheat oven to 350°. Cook pasta according to package directions; drain. In medium skillet cook onion in 1 tablespoon butter over medium heat about 5 minutes or until tender, stirring occasionally. Remove from heat; set aside.

In bowl whisk together eggs, milk, seasoning, ½ teaspoon salt, ¼ teaspoon black pepper, and crushed red pepper. Stir in chicken, Monterey Jack cheese, artichokes, spinach, tomatoes, half of the Parmesan, cooked pasta, and onion. Transfer to 3-quart rectangular baking dish.

Bake, covered, 20 minutes. In small bowl combine remaining Parmesan, bread crumbs, paprika, and melted butter. Sprinkle mixture over pasta. Bake, uncovered, 10 minutes more or until golden.

Turkey Hash

Yields 10 servings

½ cup butter
½ cup flour
4 cups milk
3 cups diced cooked turkey
½ cup finely diced cooked potatoes
½ cup finely diced cooked carrots
½ cup finely diced cooked celery
Salt and pepper
Parmesan cheese (optional)

Melt butter in a medium saucepan. Add flour and stir to blend evenly. Add milk gradually, beating well as you do to keep the mixture smooth, until all milk is added. Add remaining ingredients. Place in a buttered casserole and bake at 350° until it bubbles. If you like, sprinkle with a little Parmesan cheese over the top.

Chicken Casserole with Water Chestnuts

8 boneless chicken breast halves
2 (8 ounce) cans of sliced water chestnuts, chopped
1 (10¾ ounce) can cream of celery soup
1 (10¾ ounce) can cream of chicken soup
1 (10¾ ounce) can cream of mushroom soup
1 cup sour cream
½ cup chopped celery
3 tubes Ritz crackers, crushed
¾ cup melted butter

Place the chicken in a large, deep skillet and add water to cover. Cook over medium heat for 30 minutes, or until tender.

Drain and cool the chicken and tear/cut into bite-size pieces. Put the chicken in a large bowl and add the 3 cans of soup, sour cream, water chestnuts, and celery; mix well. Spread the chicken mixture in a greased 13 x 9-inch pan. Mix the crackers and butter, and cover the casserole with the crumbs. Bake at 350° for 30 minutes, or until bubbly.

Note: Sliced almonds may be used instead of the water chestnuts. This casserole may also be prepared in advance and refrigerated or frozen. Thaw the frozen casserole in the refrigerator overnight before baking.

Firecracker Enchilada Casserole

Yields 8-10 servings

2 pounds ground beef
1 large onion, chopped
2 tablespoons chili powder
2-3 teaspoons ground cumin
1 teaspoon salt
1 (15 ounce) can ranch-style beans
6 frozen corn tortillas, thawed
1½ cups (6 ounce) shredded Monterey Jack cheese
1½ cups (6 ounce) shredded cheddar cheese
1 (10 ounce) can tomatoes and green chiles
1 (10.75 ounce) can cream of mushroom soup, undiluted

Cook ground beef and onion in a large skillet until meat is brown and onion is tender; discard pan drippings. Add chili powder, cumin, and salt; stir well. Cook meat mixture over low heat 10 minutes. Spoon meat mixture into a 9x13x2-inch baking pan. Layer beans, tortillas, and cheese over meat mixture. Pour tomato liquid over cheese; chop tomatoes, and spread tomatoes and chiles over cheese. Spread soup over all. Cover baking pan; refrigerate overnight. Bake, uncovered at 350° for 1 hour.

Mexican Beef and Cornbread Pie

Yields 6 servings

1 pound very lean sirloin
1 large onion, chopped
2 large tomatoes, chopped
1 (10 ounce) package frozen whole kernel corn
1 large green pepper, chopped
1 teaspoon ground cumin
1 teaspoon chili powder
½ teaspoon salt (optional)
1 tablespoon Worcestershire sauce
1 cup reduced-sodium chicken or beef broth

Topping:
1½ cups yellow cornmeal
3½ cups water
¼ teaspoon salt (optional)
1 tablespoon margarine

Preheat oven to 400°. Heat nonstick skillet over medium high heat. Add beef, sauté until no longer pink, 5 minutes. Pour into a paper-towel-lined strainer, drain. Return beef to skillet; add onions and cook until translucent, 3 minutes. Add remaining ingredients. Simmer uncovered 20 minutes. Topping: Combine all ingredients in saucepan; bring to boil, stirring constantly. Cook until thickened, 3 minutes.

Place beef mixture in 2-quart baking dish. Spoon on cornmeal mixture, spreading to cover. Bake uncovered 30 to 40 minutes until topping is golden.

Easy Spaghetti Meat Sauce for 4

1 pound ground beef
1 (8 ounce) can tomato sauce
1 cup water
2 tablespoons dried onion flakes
2 teaspoons Worcestershire sauce
½ teaspoon garlic powder
¼ teaspoon pepper
1 (14 ounce) jar spaghetti sauce
Grated Parmesan cheese

Brown ground beef in a small Dutch oven, stirring until it crumbles; drain well. Stir in tomato sauce, water, dried onion flakes, Worcestershire sauce, garlic powder, and pepper. Bring to boil over medium heat. Cover, reduce heat, and simmer 20 minutes, stirring occasionally. Cook spaghetti according to the package directions, and drain. Spoon meat sauce over cooked spaghetti, and sprinkle with Parmesan cheese.

Note: Sauce can be frozen in an airtight container up to 3 months.

Easy Spaghetti Sauce for 25

6 pounds of ground beef
3 (15 ounce) cans tomato sauce
4 cups water
¾ cup dried onion flakes
¼ cup Worcestershire sauce
1 tablespoon garlic powder
1½ teaspoon pepper
3 (28 ounce) jars spaghetti sauce
3 (16 ounce) packages spaghetti, uncooked
Grated Parmesan cheese

Brown ground beef in an 8-quart Dutch oven, stirring until it crumbles; drain well. Stir in tomato sauce, water, dried onion flakes, Worcestershire sauce, garlic powder, and pepper. Bring to boil over medium heat. Cover, reduce heat, and simmer 20 minutes, stirring occasionally. Cook spaghetti according to the package directions, and drain. Spoon meat sauce over cooked spaghetti, and sprinkle with Parmesan cheese.

Note: Sauce can be frozen in an airtight container up to 3 months.

Hamburger-Rice Skillet

Yields 6 servings

1 pound ground chuck
1 small onion, chopped
1 small green bell pepper, chopped
1 (10 ounce) can mild diced tomatoes and green chiles
1½ cup water
1 cup uncooked long-grain rice
1 (1.25 ounce) envelope mild taco seasoning mix
½ teaspoon salt
2 cup chopped lettuce
3 green onions, chopped
1 tomato, chopped
1 avocado, sliced
1 (2¼ ounce) can sliced olives, drained
1 cup Mexican cheese blend
Tortilla chips
Salsa

Cook first 3 ingredients in a large skillet over medium-high heat, stirring until beef crumbles and is no longer pink; drain.

Stir in tomato and green chiles and next four ingredients. Cook, covered, over medium heat 15 minutes, stirring occasionally. Uncover and cook 15 more minutes; remove from heat.

Sprinkle lettuce and next 5 ingredients over hamburger mixture. Stand tortilla chips around edge of skillet. Serve with chips and salsa.

Boneless Rib Rubbed with Garlic and Rosemary and Red Wine Mushroom Sauce

1 boneless rib-eye roast (about 5 pounds), left at
room temperature for 2 hours before cooking
2 tablespoons olive oil
1 tablespoon salt
2 tablespoons ground black pepper (grind whole
peppercorns in a blender)
8 large garlic cloves, minced
2 tablespoons minced, fresh rosemary, plus ½ teaspoon for the sauce
2 (10 ounce) packages baby bella or white mushrooms, sliced
1 cup chicken broth
¾ cup red wine
1 tablespoon Dijon mustard
1 teaspoon cornstarch dissolved in 2 tablespoons of water

Adjust oven rack to center position and heat oven to 250°. Heat a 12-inch skillet over medium-high flame. Rub roast on all sides with oil, salt and pepper. Turn on exhaust fan, add roast to hot skillet, and brown on all sides, about 10 minutes total. Transfer roast to a plate. When cool, rub with garlic and rosemary.

Pour off all but 2 tablespoons of the beef drippings. Add mushrooms to hot skillet and sauté until browned, about 8 minutes. Mix broth, wine and mustard; add to mushrooms. Simmer to blend flavors, about 3 minutes. Pour sauce into a bowl and set aside.

Set a wire rack over the skillet, and set roast on a rack (or use a regular roasting pan with a v-rack). Slow-roast in oven 2½ to 3 hours, until meat reaches an internal temperature of 135° for medium-rare or 140° for medium.

Transfer roast to a cutting board and remove rack from skillet or pan. Pour off excess fat, if any. Set skillet or pan over medium-high heat, return mushroom sauce to pan, and heat to a simmer. Stir in cornstarch and simmer until sauce thickens slightly, about a minute. Carve meat and serve with sauce.

Braised Short Ribs

4½ pounds 3-inch long beef short ribs
Coarse kosher salt
2 cups dry red wine
1 (14.5 ounce) can diced tomatoes in juice
1 (6 ounce) package sliced button mushrooms
½ cup finely chopped onion
6 garlic cloves, peeled
6 fresh Italian parsley sprigs
2 bay leaves
Crusty bread

Sprinkle ribs with coarse salt and pepper. Place in even layer in slow cooker. Add next 7 ingredients, cover, and cook on low heat until meat is tender, about 8 hours. Spoon fat off top of sauce and pour sauce over ribs. Serve with bread.

Chicken-Fried Steak

2¼ teaspoons salt, divided
1¾ teaspoons black pepper, divided
4 (4 ounce) cube steaks
38 saltine crackers (one sleeve), crushed
1¼ cups all-purpose flour, divided
½ teaspoon ground red pepper
½ teaspoon baking powder
4¾ cups milk, divided
2 large eggs
3½ cups peanut oil
Garnish: Chopped fresh parsley

Sprinkle ¼ teaspoon salt and ¼ teaspoon black pepper evenly over steaks. Combine cracker crumbs, 1 cup flour, 1 teaspoon black pepper, red pepper, and baking powder. Whisk together ¾ cup milk and eggs. Dredge steaks in cracker mixture; dip in milk mixture; and dredge again in cracker mixture.

Pour oil into a 12-inch skillet; heat to 360°. (Do not use a nonstick skillet.) Fry steaks 3-4 minutes. Turn and fry 2-3 minutes or until golden brown. Remove steaks to a wire rack in a jelly-roll pan. Keep steaks warm in a 225° oven. Carefully drain hot oil, reserving cooked bits and 1 tablespoon drippings in skillet.

Whisk together remaining 4 cups milk, ¼ cup flour, remaining 1 teaspoon salt, and remaining 1 teaspoon black pepper. Add milk mixture to reserved drippings in skillet; cook, whisking constantly, over medium-high heat 10-12 minutes or until thickened. Serve gravy with steaks. Garnish, if desired.

Slow-Cooker Pot Roast

2 tablespoons unsalted butter
1 tablespoon sunflower oil
1 large onion, cut into wedges
3-pound boneless top round or rump roast
3 carrots, peeled and thinly sliced
3 medium white potatoes, cubed
2 bay leaves
½ teaspoon salt
2 envelopes (1.4 ounce each) onion soup mix
1 tablespoon cornstarch

Heat butter and sunflower oil in a large skillet. Add the onion and beef. Brown beef on all sides. Transfer beef and onion to a slow cooker.

Arrange carrots, potatoes, and bay leaves around beef. Sprinkle with salt. In a heatproof bowl or measuring cup, combine the soup mix with 3 cups boiling water, stirring until smooth.

Pour the soup mixture over the beef and vegetables in a slow cooker. Cover and cook on high until the meat is very tender, about 3 ½ hours.

In a medium saucepan, combine cornstarch and about 1 tablespoon water; stir to form a paste. Add 2 cups hot liquid from the slow cooker and bring to a boil, stirring until the gravy has thickened. Slice the beef and serve with vegetables and gravy.

Chapter 7

Vegetables

Corn and Basil Tart

Yields 8 servings

⅓ cup butter, softened
2 tablespoons sugar
½ teaspoon salt
3 eggs
⅔ cup all-purpose flour
1 cup half-and-half or light cream
1½ cups fresh corn kernels (about 3 ears)
½ cup coarsely snipped fresh basil
½ teaspoon salt
¼ teaspoon ground black pepper
Chopped tomato and basil (optional)
⅔ cup yellow cornmeal

For cornmeal crust, in medium bowl beat butter with electric mixer on medium to high speed for 30 seconds. Add sugar and ½ teaspoon salt. Beat until combined. Beat 1 egg until combined. Add in cornmeal and as much of the flour as you can with the mixer. Stir in any remaining flour. Form dough in a ball and wrap in plastic. Chill 30 to 60 minutes or until easy to handle.

Preheat oven to 350°. Pat dough onto bottom and sides of 9-inch tart pan with removable bottom. Press evenly onto bottom and sides with a small glass. Line pastry with double thickness of foil and bake 10 minutes. Bake 4 to 6 minutes more. Meanwhile, in a medium bowl, whisk together 2 eggs and half-and-half. Stir in corn, basil, ½ teaspoon salt, and pepper. Pour into pastry shell. Bake 35 to 40 minutes or until set. Let stand 10 minutes. Remove sides of pan to serve. Sprinkle with tomato and additional basil.

Crunch Fried Green Tomatoes

Yields 4 to 6 servings

½ cup matzo meal
1 teaspoon kosher salt
½ teaspoon ground red pepper
½ teaspoon sugar
4 to 5 large green tomatoes (about 2 pounds) cut into ½ inch-thick slices
2 large eggs, lightly beaten
Vegetable oil
Kosher salt (optional)

Combine first 4 ingredients in a shallow dish.

Dip tomatoes into eggs, allowing excess to drip off. Dredge in matzo mixture, pressing it into the surfaces. Place on a wax paper-lined baking sheet.

Pour oil to a depth of ½ inch into a large deep cast-iron or heavy skillet. Heat over medium heat to 360°. Fry tomatoes in batches, 3 to 4 minutes on each side or until golden. Drain on paper towels. Sprinkle with additional salt, if desired. Serve immediately.

Caramelized Sweet Onions

4 pounds sweet onions, chopped (about 12 cups)
1 teaspoon chopped fresh or ½ teaspoon dried thyme
2 tablespoon olive oil
½ teaspoon salt

Cook onion and thyme in hot oil in a large deep skillet over medium heat, stirring often, 35 to 40 minutes or until caramel colored. Remove from heat. Stir in salt.

Store cooked onions in a zip-top plastic freezer bag or an airtight container in refrigerator up to 1 week or freeze up to 2 months.

Heirloom Tomato Gratin

1 clove garlic, cut in half
3 tablespoons extra-virgin olive oil
1 large vidalia onion, chopped
½ teaspoon grated orange zest
3 tablespoons orange juice
2 teaspoons honey
1 tablespoon fresh thyme, chopped
4 pounds mixed heirloom tomatoes, thickly sliced
½ teaspoon each salt and pepper
2 cups fresh bread crumbs
¼ cup grated Pecorino Romano cheese

Heat oven to 425°. You'll need a shallow 2-2½ quart baking dish or gratin dish.

Vigorously rub inside of dish with garlic. Discard garlic. Brush dish with 1 tablespoon oil to coat.

Heat 1½ tablespoons oil in a large skillet over medium-low heat. Add onion and cook 15 minutes, stirring often, just until translucent and tender, but not browned. Remove from heat; stir in orange zest and juice, honey and ½ teaspoon thyme.

Scatter half over bottom of prepared dish; top with half the tomatoes and season with half the salt and pepper. Overlap tomato slices to fit.

Asparagus Vinaigrette

Yields 6-8 servings

1 bunch fresh asparagus
2 tablespoons butter
2 tablespoons oil
3 tablespoons minced onion
2 tablespoons vinegar
1 teaspoon salt
Fresh ground pepper to taste
Pimiento
Hard-boiled egg yolk

Steam asparagus, or if you do not have a steamer, use a skillet half-full of water and ½ teaspoon salt and bring to boil. Add asparagus and cook until tender. Remove from burner and drain. Place in a 7x11 glass dish, placing the spears in the same direction. Put all other ingredients, except pimiento and egg yolk, in a glass cup. Stir and cover with wax paper and microwave about 45 seconds. Stir and taste. Adjust seasonings if needed. Pour over asparagus and let it marinate. Before serving, decorate with pimiento and grated egg yolk.

Asparagus with Cream Sauce

Yields 6 servings

2 pounds fresh asparagus
¼ cup butter
¼ cup flour
¾ cup milk
2 eggs (hard boiled and minced)
2 tablespoons lemon juice

Cook asparagus and keep warm. Make cream sauce the old fashion way, stirring constantly or make it my way. Put all sauce ingredients in a microwave dish. Stir well. Microwave on high 3 minutes. Stir and cook another minute or 2. Stir and taste. Adjust seasoning if necessary.

Put asparagus in serving dish and sprinkle with lemon juice.

Put minced eggs in sauce and pour over asparagus or put in gravy boat and serve sauce along with the asparagus.

Leek and Asparagus Frittata

2 teaspoons butter
1 cup chopped leeks (white and pale green parts only)
1 12-ounce bunch thin asparagus, trimmed, cut on diagonal into 1-inch pieces (about 2 ½ cups)
1 cup sliced stemmed shitake mushrooms
8 large eggs
1 cup diced Fontina cheese, divided
½ teaspoon salt
½ teaspoon ground pepper
¼ cup grated Parmesan cheese

Preheat broiler. Melt butter in heavy broiler-proof 10-inch diameter nonstick skillet over medium heat. Add leeks and sauté 4 minutes. Add asparagus and shitake mushrooms, sprinkle lightly with salt, and sauté until tender, about 6 minutes. Whisk eggs, ¾ cup Fontina cheese, ½ teaspoon salt, and ½ teaspoon pepper in medium bowl. Add egg mixture to skillet; fold gently to combine. Cook until almost set. Sprinkle with remaining ¼ cup Fontina cheese and Parmesan cheese. Broil until frittata is puffed and cheese begins to turn golden, about 3 minutes. Cut into wedges and serve. May add chicken or shrimp to make this into a meal.

Green Bean Bundles

1 cup firmly packed brown sugar
½ cup butter
2 teaspoons garlic powder
3 (14½ ounce) whole green beans
1 pound sliced peppered bacon

Combine first 4 ingredients in small pan over high heat.

When butter melts remove and set aside. Bundle 6 or 7 beans together. Wrap with 1 piece of bacon. Place on pan or baking sheet. Spoon butter mixture over bundles. Cover and marinate overnight. Preheat oven at 350°. Uncover beans and bake for 40 minutes.

Lima Bean and Peas

1 (10 ounce) package frozen green baby lima beans
1 (10 ounce) package frozen green peas
1 small onion, minced
¾ stick of butter or margarine
1 (4 ounce) can sliced mushrooms, drained
1 tablespoon sweet basil
¾ cup milk or half-and-half
1 teaspoon sugar
1 can sliced water chestnuts or slivered almonds
Salt and pepper to taste

Cook peas and beans according to package directions. Drain each. Cook onion slightly in butter, add half-and-half or milk. Then add other ingredients and simmer about 10 minutes.

Sweet and Sour Green Beans

3 cans French cut green beans
6 slices bacon
1 medium onion, diced
3 tablespoons pimiento
¼ cup vinegar
¼ cup sugar
1 teaspoon salt
Coarse ground black pepper
¼ cup toasted almonds

Drain beans and fry bacon until crisp. Remove the bacon to a paper towel to drain. To the bacon grease, add the vinegar, onion, sugar, pepper, and salt. Let boil. Taste for seasoning. Pour over beans and cook approximately 30-45 minutes. Add pimiento, almonds, and crumbled bacon just before serving.

Corn Vegetable Medley

Yields 6 servings
1 (10¾ ounce) can Campbell's Golden Corn Soup
½ cup milk
2 cup broccoli florets
1 cup sliced carrots
1 cup cauliflower
1½ cup shredded cheddar cheese (optional)

In saucepan, heat soup and milk to boiling, stirring often. Stir in vegetables.

Return to boiling. Cover. Cook over low heat 20 minutes or until vegetables are tender, stirring often. Stir in cheese. Heat through.

If desired, substitute 1 bag (16 ounce) frozen broccoli, carrots and cauliflower for fresh vegetables. Reduce cooking time to 15 minutes.

Eggplant Ole

Yields 6 servings

1 medium eggplant (about 1 pound)
2 tablespoons water
2 medium tomatoes, seeded and chopped (2 cups)
1 (4 ounce) can diced green chili peppers, drained
½ teaspoon dried oregano, crushed
¼ teaspoon ground cumin
¼ teaspoon pepper
¼ cup shredded Monterey Jack cheese
Snipped cilantro or parsley (optional)

Rinse the eggplant and cut off the top. Peel, if desired, and cut crosswise into ½-inch slices. Place eggplant in a 12x7x2-inch microwave-safe baking dish, overlapping the slices as needed. Add water. Cover with vented microwave-safe plastic wrap. Microwave on 100 percent for 5 to 7 minutes or until the eggplant is tender, turning the dish once. Drain.

In a mixing bowl, combine tomatoes, chili peppers, oregano, cumin, salt, and pepper. Top eggplant with the tomato mixture. Cook, uncovered on high for 1 to 2 minutes or until heated through. Sprinkle cheese over all. Let stand, covered, for 2 to 3 minutes or until cheese is melted. Sprinkle with cilantro.

Gourmet Eggplant

Yields 8 servings

1 large eggplant, peeled and thinly sliced
2 eggs, well beaten
1½ cup fine cracker crumbs
Hot salad oil
2 (8 ounce) cans tomato sauce
½ teaspoon Worcestershire sauce
1 teaspoon whole oregano
1 (8 ounce) package pasteurized processed American cheese slices
Salt and pepper to taste

Dip eggplant slices in egg, and coat with cracker crumbs. Brown slowly in hot oil. Drain. Combine tomato sauce, Worcestershire sauce, salt, pepper and oregano. Blend well.

Place ¼ of eggplant slices in a lightly greased 2-quart casserole. Top with ¼ of cheese. Spoon ¼ of sauce mixture over cheese. Repeat layers until all ingredients are used, ending with sauce.

Cover and bake at 350° for 50 to 55 minutes.

Mushroom Pie on the sideboard during a dinner
at the Tucker house on Main Street.

Mushroom Pie

Yields 4 to 6 servings

Pastry for a one-crust pie
1 small onion, peeled and minced
1 cup grated cheddar cheese
1 (6 ounce) can mushrooms, drained
1 cup light cream
½ cup milk
3 eggs
½ teaspoon Worcestershire sauce
½ teaspoon salt
Dash pepper
Paprika

Prepare pastry, your own or mix and fit into a 9-inch pie pan. Preheat oven to 350°. Chop onion very fine and sprinkle onion, grated cheese and drained mushrooms over bottom of the unbaked pie shell. Heat cream and milk together until a film shines over the surface. Remove from heat. Beat eggs until light and pour in heated milk very slowly. Season with Worcestershire sauce, salt, pepper and pour into pie shell. Sprinkle top with paprika and bake 40 minutes or until a knife comes out dry when tested in center of the pie. Serve immediately.

Bermuda Onion Casserole

Yields 4 servings

2 Bermuda onions, thinly sliced
1 cup sour cream
3 tablespoons crumbs or cornflake crumbs
Salt and pepper to taste
Paprika

Spread onion slices in a greased 9x9 casserole. Spread seasoned sour cream evenly over onions. Top with crumbs and sprinkle with paprika.
Bake 30-35 minutes at 375°.

Grilled Onions

Yields 6 servings

¼ cup olive oil
¼ cup balsamic vinegar
1 tablespoon chopped fresh parsley
1 tablespoon chopped fresh thyme
1 tablespoon chopped fresh basil
½ teaspoon salt and pepper each
4 large sweet onions

Preheat grill to 350 to 400° heat. Whisk together first 7 ingredients. Cut onions into ½-inch thick slices. Brush with herb mixture. Grill onions. Cover with grill lid, 10 minutes each side or until golden brown. Remove from grill. Pour remaining herb mixture over onions, and serve immediately.

Peppers Stuffed with Macaroni and Ham

6 large green peppers
2½ cup cooked macaroni
1½ cup chopped ham
½ cup cracker crumbs
1½ cup grated American or mild cheddar cheese
1 (8 ounce) can tomato sauce mixed with ½ cup water

Cut peppers in half and remove stems and seeds. Boil 10 minutes in salted water. Drain and place in large, flat baking dish. Combine macaroni, ham, and crumbs. Add half the cheese and half the tomato sauce-water mixture. Stir well and spoon into pepper halves. Sprinkle remaining cheese on top and drizzle on the remaining tomato sauce and water mixture. Cover loosely with foil and bake 30 minutes. Remove foil and bake 30 minutes longer.

Creamy Mashed Potatoes

Yields 4 servings

3 tablespoons butter
1 large garlic clove, minced
1 (22 ounce) bag frozen mashed potatoes
2⅓ cups milk
½ teaspoon salt
¼ teaspoon pepper

Melt butter in a small saucepan over medium-low heat. Add garlic and sauté until tender. Remove from saucepan and set aside.

Prepare mashed potatoes in saucepan according to package directions, using 2⅓ cups milk and stirring with wire whisk.

Stir in garlic mixture, salt, and pepper. Let potatoes stand 5 minutes before serving.

Cheddar Baked Potato Slices

Yields 6 servings

1 (10¾ ounce) can Campbell's Cream of Mushroom soup
½ teaspoon paprika
½ teaspoon pepper
4 medium baking potatoes cut into ¼-inch slices (about 4 cups)
1 cup shredded cheddar cheese

In a small bowl, combine soup, paprika, and pepper.

In greased 2-quart oblong baking dish, arrange potatoes in overlapping rows. Sprinkle with cheese. Spoon soup mixture over cheese.

Cover with foil. Bake 10 minutes or until potatoes are fork-tender.

Oven Parmesan Chips

Yields 4-6 servings

4 medium unpeeled baking potatoes
¼ cup butter or margarine, melted
1 tablespoon finely minced onion
½ teaspoon salt
¼ teaspoon pepper
Dash paprika
2 tablespoons grated Parmesan cheese

Cut potatoes into ¼-inch slices. Place on a greased baking sheet in a single layer. Mix butter, onion, salt, pepper, and paprika. Brush on one side of potatoes then turn and brush the other side. Bake at 425° for 15-20 minutes or until potatoes are tender and golden. Sprinkle with Parmesan cheese. Serve immediately.

Roasted Potatoes

Yields 8 servings

3 pounds baby new potatoes
2 teaspoons olive oil
Salt and freshly ground pepper
3 unpeeled garlic cloves
Fresh thyme or rosemary sprigs

Preheat oven to 400°. Rub potatoes with oil and sprinkle with salt and pepper. Arrange potatoes in a baking pan and scatter garlic cloves and herb sprigs around them.

Roast for 25 to 40 minutes, shaking pan from time to time, until potatoes are tender. Serve warm.

Roasted Potato Medley

2 sweet potatoes
4 Yukon Gold potatoes
8 new potatoes
¼ cup plus 2 tablespoons olive oil
1 teaspoon dried tarragon
⅛ teaspoon salt
⅛ teaspoon pepper

Preheat oven to 425°. Peel and cube the sweet potatoes and Yukon Gold potatoes. Scrub the new potatoes and cut into cubes.

Place the potatoes in a large saucepan. Add enough lightly salted water to cover the potatoes. Bring to a boil and cook the potatoes for 3 minutes. Drain thoroughly.

Spread the potatoes in a single layer on a large nonstick baking sheet.

Drizzle the potatoes with olive oil and sprinkle with tarragon, salt, and pepper. Roast the potatoes until browned and crisp, about 25 minutes. Serve immediately.

Sweet Potatoes

6 medium sweet potatoes
¾ cup white sugar
1 tablespoon cornstarch
½ teaspoon salt
2 tablespoon grated orange rind
1 cup fresh orange juice
3 tablespoons butter

Peel and slice potatoes, slice in ⅛-inch pieces. Place in casserole. Put remaining ingredients in saucepan and cook over medium heat, stirring until slightly thick. Pour over sweet potato slices. Bake covered at 325° to 350° for an hour or until the potatoes are tender.

Sweet Potatoes in Orange Shells

Sweet Potatoes in Orange Shells

6 small oranges
4 large sweet potatoes
4 tablespoon frozen orange juice concentrate
3 tablespoons melted butter
½ teaspoon salt
1 teaspoon orange flavor
¼ teaspoon black pepper
¼ cup white sugar

Topping:
¼ cup brown sugar
3 tablespoons melted butter
1 teaspoon cinnamon
3 tablespoons chopped walnuts or pecans

Cut oranges in half. Squeeze juice and save for breakfast.
Use a serrated fruit spoon to get the membrane out of the orange halves.
Boil the sweet potatoes until tender. Let cool slightly. Peel and mash with the next 5 ingredients. Taste and add seasoning as needed. If needed, add more sugar. Fill orange halves.

Mix next 4 ingredients and put on top of potatoes. Bake at 350° approximately 20 minutes. Turn on broiler the last 3-5 minutes. Miniature marshmallows may be added around edge.

Spinach-Stuffed Squash

Yields 8 servings

8 medium-size yellow squash
1 chicken-flavored bouillon cube
1 (10 ounce) package frozen chopped spinach
¼ cup low-fat cottage cheese
1 tablespoon Parmesan cheese
1 large egg, beaten
¼ teaspoon seasoned salt
¼ teaspoon onion salt
¼ teaspoon coarsely ground black pepper
3 tablespoons bread crumbs
Paprika
Vegetable cooking spray

Wash squash thoroughly. Drop in boiling water with bouillon cube. Cover and simmer 8 to 10 minutes or until tender but still firm. Drain and cool slightly. Trim off stems. Cut squash in half lengthwise. Scoop out pulp, leaving firm shells. Mash the pulp.

Cook spinach according to package directions. Drain well and add to squash pulp. Add cottage cheese and mix well. Stir in next 5 ingredients. Spoon into squash shells.

Sprinkle squash with bread crumbs and paprika. Place on a baking sheet with cooking spray. Cover with foil and bake at 325° for 30 minutes.

Sautéed Cherry Tomatoes with Garlic and Basil

Yields 8 servings

2 tablespoons olive oil, divided
2 pints cherry or grape tomatoes (can combine red and yellow varieties)
Salt and freshly ground pepper
2 garlic cloves, minced
1 tablespoon minced fresh basil
1 teaspoon sugar

Heat 1 tablespoon olive oil in a 12-inch skillet over medium-high flame until it just starts to smoke. Add tomatoes, and season with salt and pepper.

Sauté, shaking the pan, until tomatoes soften and skins just begin to wrinkle, about 2 minutes. Stir in the garlic and continue to shake the pan until garlic is fragrant. Take off heat. Stir in the basil and remaining 1 tablespoon olive oil, then serve.

Vegetable Medley

Yields 4 servings

1½ cup broccoli florets
1½ cup sliced zucchini
½ cup sweet red pepper
½ cups sliced water chestnuts
¼ cup sliced green onions
2 teaspoons chicken-flavored bouillon granules
2 tablespoons margarine
Salt and pepper
Pinch of sugar

Combine first 5 ingredients in a 2-quart casserole. Sprinkle with bouillon granules and toss. Dot with margarine. Cover with plastic wrap, venting one corner. Microwave at high for 4 minutes, turning dish ½ turn after 2 minutes. Let stand, covered for 5 minutes.

Mushroom Wild Rice

4 cups water
1 cup uncooked wild rice
1 teaspoon butter or margarine
1½ teaspoons salt, divided
8 bacon strips, diced
2 cups sliced fresh mushrooms
1 large onion, chopped
1 medium green pepper, chopped
1 medium sweet red pepper, chopped
1 celery rib, thinly sliced
1 (14½ ounce) can beef broth
2 tablespoons cornstarch
¼ cup cold water
½ cup slivered almonds

In a large saucepan, bring water, wild rice, butter, and ½ teaspoon salt to a boil. Reduce heat. Cover and simmer for 40 minutes. Stir in brown rice. Cover and simmer 25-30 minutes longer, or until rice is tender. Meanwhile, in a large skillet, cook bacon until crisp. Remove bacon to paper towels. Drain, reserving 2 tablespoons drippings. In the drippings, sauté mushrooms, onion, peppers and celery until tender. Stir in broth and remaining salt. Bring to a boil. Combine the cornstarch and cold water until smooth. Stir into the mushroom mixture. Cook and stir for 2 minutes or until thickened and bubbly. Stir in almonds and bacon. Drain rice. Add mushroom mixture. Transfer to a greased 13x9x2-inch baking dish. Cover and bake at 350° for 25 minutes. Uncover. Bake 5-10 minutes longer or until heated through.

Barbequed Butter Beans

Yields 8-10 servings

2 (10 ounce) boxes frozen butter beans, cooked and drained
6 slices bacon, crumbled
¾ cup minced onions
⅓ cup minced celery
⅓ cup bell pepper, minced
2 large garlic cloves, minced
¼ cup barbeque sauce
2 cups drained canned tomatoes
2 tablespoons brown sugar
¼ cup flour
Salt and pepper to taste

Preheat oven to 350°. Fry the bacon and then sauté the minced vegetables in the bacon grease. Add the flour, tomatoes, salt, pepper, and brown sugar. Add the cooked and drained butter beans. Adjust the seasonings, pour into casserole, and top with crumbled bacon. Bake until bubbly. This freezes well.

Picnic Baked Beans

Yields 6 servings

1 (16 ounce) can pork and beans
1 (15½ ounce) can kidney beans
1 (17 ounce) can lima beans, drained
½ pound Frankfurters cut in 1½-inch pieces
½ cup firmly packed brown sugar
¼ cup ketsup
2 tablespoons chopped onion
½ teaspoon salt
⅛ teaspoon garlic salt

Combine all ingredients; spoon into a lightly greased 2-quart casserole. Cover and bake at 375° for 35 minutes.

Classic Green Bean Bake

1 (10¾-ounce) can Campbell's cream of mushroom soup
½ cup milk
1 teaspoon soy sauce
Dash of pepper
2 packages (9 ounce each) frozen cut green beans, cooked and drained
1 can (2.8 ounce) French fried onions

In a 1½-quart casserole, combine soup, milk, soy sauce and pepper. Add beans and ½ can of onions.

Conventional: Bake at 350° for 25 minutes or until hot and bubbling. Stir. Top with remaining onions. Bake 5 minutes more.

Microwave: Cover with lid. Microwave on high 7 minutes or until hot and bubbling. Stir halfway through heating. Top with remaining onions. Microwave, uncovered 1 minute more.

Broccoli 'N Mushroom Bake

½ cup Miracle Whip salad dressing
3 tablespoons flour
¼ teaspoon salt
⅛ teaspoon pepper
1 cup milk
1 (4 ounce) can mushrooms, drained
2 tablespoons sliced pimiento, drained
2 (10 ounce) packages frozen broccoli spears, cooked and drained
¼ cup (5) crushed wheat crackers
1 tablespoon melted butter

Combine salad dressing, flour and seasonings. Gradually add milk. Cook, stirring constantly, over low heat, until thickened. Remove from heat; stir in mushrooms and pimento. Arrange broccoli in 12x8 baking dish; top with salad dressing mixture. Toss crumbs with margarine; sprinkle over casserole. Bake at 350° for 25-30 minutes.

Make ahead: prepare as directed except for baking. Cover; refrigerate several hours or overnight. When ready to serve, bake uncovered at 350° for 30 minutes.

Carrot Casserole

Yields 6 servings

3 cups canned sliced carrots
4 slices bacon, crumbled
1 tablespoon minced onion
½ teaspoon salt
¼ teaspoon pepper
3 tablespoons brown sugar
3 tablespoons melted butter

Drain carrots. Combine all ingredients except sugar and butter. Grease casserole. Sprinkle sugar and butter on top and cover to cook. Bake in 375° oven for 25 minutes.

Zesty Carrots

Yields 6 sevings

6-8 cooked carrots, cut in length-wise strips
¼ cup water or carrot juice
2 tablespoons grated onion
2 tablespoons horseradish (optional)
½ cup mayonnaise
¼ cup bread or cracker crumbs
1 teaspoon oleo
Dash of paprika
Minced parsley for garnish

Mix water or carrot juice, onion, horseradish, and mayonnaise and pour over carrots. Top with mixture of bread or cracker crumbs, oleo and paprika. Bake in 375° oven for 15-20 minutes. Garnish with minced parsley.

Crisp Celery Casserole

2 cup chopped celery
1 cup sliced water chestnuts
1 cup cream of chicken soup
32 Ritz crackers, crushed
3½ ounces slivered almonds
¼ pound butter
Pinch of sugar

Boil celery in sugar and salt water for 7 minutes. Drain well. Place celery, chestnuts and soup in a casserole dish. Sauté almonds in butter. Mix with crackers. Put on top of celery mixture. Bake at 350° for 30 minutes.

Corn and Broccoli Casserole

2 packages frozen cut broccoli
2 cans cream-style corn
2 eggs, well beaten
2 cups Town House cracker crumbs
½ cup shredded sharp cheddar cheese
1 teaspoon salt
½ teaspoon pepper
1 teaspoon garlic salt
6 tablespoons butter, melted
Pinch of sugar

Preheat oven to 350°. Cook broccoli and drain thoroughly. Combine with corn. Add remaining ingredients, leaving cheese for topping. Place in a casserole and bake for 45 minutes to 1 hour. Top with cheese during last 15 minutes of baking.

This recipe is from my niece Linda Frazer who lives in Shawnee, Kansas.

Corn Casserole

Yields 8 servings

2 (16½ ounce) cans yellow cream-style corn
2 cups shredded cheddar cheese
1 (4 ounce) can chopped green chiles, drained
½ cup finely chopped onions
1 cup milk
2 large eggs, lightly beaten
1 cup yellow cornmeal
1½ teaspoons garlic salt
½ teaspoon baking soda

Combine first 6 ingredients in a large bowl. Combine cornmeal and remaining ingredients. Stir into corn mixture. Pour into a lightly greased 11x7x1½-inch baking dish. Bake at 350° for 50 minutes.

Corn Pudding

Yields 8 servings

1 can whole-kernel corn, drained
1 can cream-style corn
3 teaspoons melted butter
1 teaspoon salt
1 teaspoon sugar
5 eggs
1 cup heavy cream
1 cup milk
1½ cups fresh, plain or buttered bread crumbs (optional)

Combine the whole and creamed corn, melted butter, salt and sugar. Lightly beat the eggs and beat in the milk and cream. Combine this with the corn mixture. Pour the mixture into a well-greased 7½x10½x2-inch baking dish. Bake at 350° and bake an additional 20 to 30 minutes and serve.

Spinach Casserole

Yields 10-12 servings

1 pound fresh spinach
1 stick butter
1 pound cottage cheese
½ pound American cheese
6 eggs
6 tablespoons flour

Beat eggs in cottage cheese. Cut American cheese and butter into small cubes and add to above. Chop spinach and sprinkle with flour and mix lightly. Add to other mixture.

Pour into greased casserole. Bake at 350° for 1 hour.

Squash Casserole

2-3 packages squash
1 medium onion, chopped
6-8 slices American cheese, grated
1 stick butter
1 can cream of mushroom soup
Ritz crackers
Salt and pepper to taste

Cook squash and onion until tender. Line baking dish with cracker crumbs. Layer ingredients. Cover with soup. Top with cracker crumbs. Bake at 350° until brown and bubbly.

Yellow & Green Squash Casserole

5 to 6 cups grated yellow and zucchini squash, mixed about equal
1 large yellow onion, diced
½ cup diced celery
1 cup grated cheddar cheese
1 to 2 cloves garlic, pressed
1 teaspoon salt
½ teaspoon fresh ground pepper
½ cup sour cream
½ cup mayonnaise
1 teaspoon curry
3 eggs beaten

Mix ingredients in order listed. Put in buttered casserole and top with cracker crumbs mixed with Parmesan cheese. Dot with butter and bake at 325-350° for 45 minutes.

Baked Zucchini Casserole

Yields 12 servings
3 pounds of zucchini, sliced in ⅛-inch pieces
1 pound grated cheddar cheese
6 whole eggs, beaten
1 cup chopped onion
1 cup chopped celery
1 cup chopped green peppers
1 tablespoon chopped fresh garlic
1 teaspoon salt
1 teaspoon white pepper
½ cup Parmesan cheese
½ cup bread crumbs
⅛ cup butter

Cook zucchini for 2 minutes in boiling water. Remove and drain. Sauté onion, celery, green pepper, and garlic in butter until tender. Remove from heat. Mix with zucchini. Add cheddar cheese, eggs, salt and pepper. Mix Parmesan cheese and bread crumbs. Place zucchini mix in a 2-inch casserole. Top with crumb mix. Bake at 275° for 1 hour. Casserole should be golden brown.

Vegetable Casserole

3 cans mixed vegetables, such as Veg-All
1 can sliced water chestnuts
1½ sticks butter or margarine
1 (16 ounce) jar Cheez Whiz
1 package Ritz crackers

Butter 2½ quart dish. Melt ½ stick butter or margarine. Pour over drained vegetables and water chestnuts. Melt Cheese Whiz and pour over the other ingredients. Cover with crushed Ritz crackers. Dot with one stick of butter or margarine. Bake at 350° for 30 minutes.

Swiss Vegetable Medley

1 large bag frozen vegetables (mixed broccoli, cauliflower and carrots)
1 cup cream of mushroom soup
1 cup shredded cheese
⅓ cup sour cream
1 cup French-fried onions

Combine ½ cup onions and ½ cup cheese and rest of ingredients. Bake at 350° for 30 minutes. Then sprinkle with remaining onions and cheese. Return to oven for 5 more minutes.

Chapter 8

Desserts: Cakes, Cookies, Cobblers, Pies & Puddings

Best-Ever Chocolate Cake

12-16 servings

¾ cup butter
3 eggs
2 cups all-purpose flour
¾ cup unsweetened cocoa powder
1 teaspoon baking soda
¾ teaspoon baking powder
½ teaspoon salt
2 cups sugar
2 teaspoons vanilla
1½ cups milk

Allow butter and eggs to stand at room temperature for 30 minutes. Lightly grease bottoms of three 8x1½-inch round cake pans. Line bottoms of pans with waxed paper. Grease and lightly flour waxed paper and sides of pans. Set pans aside.

Preheat oven to 350º. In a medium bowl, stir together the flour, cocoa powder, baking soda, baking powder, and salt; set aside.

In a large mixing bowl, beat butter with an electric mixer on medium to high speed for 30 seconds. Gradually add sugar, about ¼ cup at a time, beating on medium speed for 3 to 4 minutes or until well mixed. Add eggs, one at a time, beating after each addition (about 1 minute total). Beat in vanilla.

Alternately add flour mixture and milk to beaten mixture, beat on low speed just until combined after each addition. Beat on medium to high speed for 20 seconds more. Spread evenly into prepared pans.

Bake for 30 to 35 minutes, or until a wooden toothpick inserted in the centers comes out clean. Cool cake layers in pans for 10 minutes. Remove from pans. Peel off waxed paper. Cool completely on wire racks.

Prepare chocolate frosting; fill and frost cake layers. If desired, top with chocolate curls and candied nuts. Store cake in the refrigerator.

Chocolate frosting: In a large saucepan, combine one 12-ounce package (2 cups) semisweet chocolate pieces and ½ cup butter; heat over low heat until melted, stirring often. Cool for 5 minutes. Stir in one 8-ounce carton sour cream. Gradually add 4 ½ cups sifted powder sugar (about 1 pound), beating on medium speed until smooth.

Hawaiian Cake

12-15 servings

1 package (18¼ ounce) yellow cake mix
1¼ cups cold milk
1 package (3.4 ounce) instant vanilla pudding mix
1 can (20 ounce) crushed pineapple, drained
1 envelope whipped topping mix
1 package (3 ounce) cream cheese, softened
¼ cup sugar
½ teaspoon vanilla extract
½ cup flaked coconut, toasted

Prepare and bake the cake according to package directions, using a greased 9x13x2-inch baking pan. Cool. In a bowl, whisk together milk and pudding mix; let stand to thicken. Stir in pineapple. Spread over cake. Prepare whipped topping mix according to package directions; set aside. In a mixing bowl, beat cream cheese, sugar, and vanilla until smooth. Beat in 1 cup whipped topping. Fold in remaining topping. Spread over pudding. Sprinkle with coconut. Cover and refrigerate for 3 hours or overnight.

Creamy Strawberry-Lemon Squares

24 servings

1½ cups graham crackers, finely crushed
½ cup sugar, divided
6 tablespoons butter or margarine, softened
2 packages (8 ounce) cream cheese, softened
3 cups milk, divided
2 packages (4 serving size) lemon flavored instant pudding & pie filling
1 tub (8 ounce) strawberry whipped topping

Mix graham cracker crumbs, ¼ cup sugar and butter until blended. Press onto bottom of 13x9-inch baking pan. Beat cream cheese, ¼ cup sugar and ¼ cup milk until blended. Spread over crust. Pour 2 ¾ cups milk into large bowl. Add pudding mixes. Blend well. Pour over cream cheese layer. Let stand 5 minutes or until thickened. Cover with whipped topping. Refrigerate 4 hours or overnight.

Fruit No-Bake Cheesecake

Yields 16 servings

1½ cups graham cracker crumbs
¼ cup (½ stick) butter, melted
2 tablespoons sugar
4 packages (8 ounce) cream cheese
½ cup sugar
1 package (12 ounce) frozen mixed berries
(strawberries, raspberries, blueberries, and blackberries), thawed and drained
1 tub whipped topping, divided

Line 9x13-inch pan with foil, with ends of foil extending over sides of pan. Mix graham cracker crumbs, butter and 2 tablespoons sugar; press firmly onto bottom of prepared pan. Refrigerate while preparing filling.

Beat cream cheese and ½ cup sugar in large bowl with electric mixer on medium speed until well blended. Smash drained berries with fork; stir into cheese mixture. Gently stir in 2 cups of the whipped topping. Spoon over crust; cover.

Refrigerate 4 hours or until firm. Use foil handles to remove cheesecake from pan before cutting into pieces to serve. Top with remaining whipped topping. Store leftover cheesecake in refrigerator.

Triple Chocolate Cake

Yields 12 servings

Cocoa
1 (18½ ounce) box deep chocolate or devil's food cake mix
1 (4 ounce) box instant chocolate pudding
¾ cup sour cream
½ cup sour cream
½ cup water
½ cup toasted chopped almonds
¼ cup mayonnaise
4 eggs
3 tablespoons almond liqueur
1 teaspoon almond extract
1 cup chocolate chips

Preheat oven to 350°. Grease 10-inch bundt pan and dust with cocoa. Place all ingredients except chocolate chips in large bowl and beat 2 minutes with electric mixer on medium speed. Mix in chocolate chips. Pour into prepared pan. Bake 50 to 55 minutes, or until cake tests done. Cool on rack 10 minutes before removing from pan. Place warm cake on serving dish and drizzle with glaze.

Glaze: Mix 1 cup powdered sugar, 3 tablespoons milk, and 1 teaspoon almond extract thoroughly in a small bowl. Let stand at room temperature until ready to glaze cake.

Double Chocolate Cheesecake

Yields 8 to 10 servings

1½ cups cream-filled chocolate sandwich cookie crumbs
(about 18 cookies)
1 (12 ounce) package semi-sweet chocolate morsels
3 (8 ounce) packages cream cheese, softened
1 (14 ounce) can sweetened condensed milk
2 teaspoons vanilla extract
4 large eggs
Ganache Topping

Press cookie crumbs into bottom and halfway up sides of a 9-inch spring-form pan; set aside.

194

Microwave chocolate morsels in a microwave-safe bowl at high 1½ minutes or until melted, stirring at 30-second intervals.

Beat cream cheese at medium speed with an electric mixer 2 minutes or until smooth. Add sweetened condensed milk and vanilla, beating at low speed just until combined. Add eggs, 1 at a time, beating at low speed just until combined after each addition. Add melted chocolate, beating just until combined. Pour cheesecake batter into prepared crust.

Bake at 300° for 1 hour and 5 minutes or just until center is set. Turn oven off. Let cheesecake stand in oven for 30 minutes with oven door closed. Remove cheesecake from oven; run a knife along outer edge of cheesecake, and cool in pan on a wire rack until room temperature. Cover and chill 8 hours.

Ganache Topping: Bring ¾ cup whipping cream to a boil in a saucepan over medium heat; quickly remove from heat, and stir 1 (6 ounce) package of semi-sweet chocolate morsels and 1 (6 ounce) milk chocolate morsels until melted and smooth. Let mixture cool (about 30 minutes) until slightly warm before pouring and spreading over cheesecake.

Fluffy Pistachio Dessert

Yields 24 servings

½ cup reduced fat margarine (70% vegetable spread), softened
1 cup all purpose flour
½ cup confectioners' sugar
½ cup chopped walnuts
First Layer:
1 (8 ounce) package fat free cream cheese, softened
1 cup (8 ounce) nonfat sour cream
1 carton (8 ounce) frozen light whipped topping, thawed
Second Layer:
3 cups cold skim milk
2 (1 ounce) packages sugar-free fat-free instant pistachio pudding mix
Topping:
1 carton (8 ounce) frozen light whipped topping, thawed

In a mixing bowl, cream the margarine. Add flour and sugar; blend until crumbly. Stir in walnuts. Press into bottom of a 13x9x2-inch baking dish coated with nonstick cooking spray. Bake at 375° for 10-12 minutes or until set. Cool. In a mixing bowl, beat cream cheese and sour cream. Fold in whipped topping. Spread over crust. In another mixing bowl, combine milk and pudding mixes; beat on low speed for 2 minutes. Spread over first layer.

Carefully spread whipped topping over second layer. Sprinkle with walnuts. Chill at least 1 hour.

Chocolate Cake

1 box cake mix (chocolate or fudge or devil's food)
1 box chocolate instant pudding mix
1 (12 ounce) package of chocolate chips
2 eggs
1¾ cups milk
⅓ cup oleo or butter, softened
3 ounces unsweetened chocolate, melted and cooled
3 cups powder sugar
½ cup sour cream
2 teaspoons vanilla

Preheat oven to 350°. Mix cake mix, pudding mix, 12 ounce package of chocolate chips, eggs, and milk for 2 minutes. Bake in a floured tube pan for 50 minutes.

Icing: Mix oleo and cooled chocolate. Blend in powdered sugar, stir in sour cream and vanilla. Mix well. After cake cools, spread over the cake.

Fresh Apple Cake

2 cups sugar
1½ cups oil
3 eggs
3 cups flour
1 teaspoon baking soda
1 teaspoon salt
2 cups apples, diced or coarsely shredded
1 cups nuts, shredded
1 teaspoon vanilla
1 cup flaked coconut

Beat together sugar, oil and eggs. In a separate bowl, mix together flour, baking soda, and salt, then add to egg mixture. Fold into apples, nuts, vanilla, and coconut. Pour into greased and floured 9x13-inch baking pan. Bake at 325-350° for 45-60 minutes. Good plain or frosted.

Applesauce Cake

3½ cups flour
2 teaspoons baking soda
½ teaspoon salt
2 teaspoons cinnamon
1 teaspoon cloves
½ teaspoon nutmeg
½ teaspoon mace
1 cup butter
2 cups sugar
2 eggs
2 cups seedless raisins
1 cup nuts, chopped
1 pound mixed candied fruits, chopped
2 cups hot applesauce

Sift first 7 ingredients together. Cream the butter and sugar in a bowl. Add the eggs and beat well. Mix the raisins, nuts, and candied fruits with flour mixture and add to the creamed mixture alternately with the applesauce. Pour into a large tube pan. Bake at 275° for 2 hours.

Cream of Coconut Cake

16 servings

2 sticks (1 cup) butter, at room temperature
1½ cups sugar
2 teaspoons baking powder
½ teaspoon baking soda
4 large eggs
1 can (15 ounce) cream of coconut (not coconut milk)
2 teaspoons vanilla extract
3 cups cake flour (not self rising)
¾ cup buttermilk
16 ounces strawberries
3 cups (1½ pints) heavy (whipping) cream
3 cups sweetened flaked coconut

Divide oven in thirds. Preheat oven to 350°. You will need 8x2-inch round cake pans coated with a non-stick cooking spray. Line bottoms with wax paper; spray paper.

Beat butter, sugar, baking powder, and baking soda in a large bowl with mixer on medium 1 minute until blended. Add eggs, one at a time, beating well after each. Add 1 cup cream of coconut and vanilla. Beat 1 minute until fluffy. On low speed, beat in flour in three additions alternating with buttermilk in two additions, just until blended. Divide batter between prepared pans, spreading evenly.

Bake 30 minutes or until wooden toothpick inserted in centers comes out clean. Cool in pans, peel off paper and cool completely.

Cut enough strawberries into ¼-inch thick slices to make 2 cups. Reserve remaining whole berries for garnish. Beat heavy cream and the remaining cream of coconut in a large bowl until stiff enough to spread. Place a cake layer on a serving platter. Spread 1 cup whipped cream, top with 1 cup sliced berries and cake layer; repeat. Frost sides and then top with remaining whipped cream. Cover sides and top with coconut. Refrigerate at least 1 hour before serving.

German Sweet Chocolate Cake

2 cups sugar
4 eggs
1 teaspoon baking soda
1 package German sweet chocolate
1 cup Crisco
2½ cups sifted flour
1 teaspoon vanilla
1 cup buttermilk
1 teaspoon salt
2 cups boiling water

Dissolve chocolate in boiling water, let cool. Cream sugar and Crisco. Add egg yolks. Beat. Add ¾ cups buttermilk alternately with flour and salt. Dissolve soda in remaining buttermilk. Add to flour mixture. Mix in chocolate and vanilla. Fold in beaten egg whites. Bake in three 9-inch pans at 350° for 25 to 30 minutes.

Icing:
½ cup whipping cream or evaporated milk
3 egg yolks
½ cup (1 stick) butter
1 cup sugar
⅛ teaspoon salt
1 egg white
1 cup nuts, chopped
1 cup coconut (1 can Bakers Angel Flake)
1 teaspoon vanilla

Cook in top of double broiler over boiling water, beating with rotary beater until thick, about 14-20 minutes. Remove from heat. Add vanilla, nuts, and coconut. Spread between layers and on top of cake.

Note: This recipe was given to me by the late Anita Guggenheim.

Orange Slice Cake

3½ cups all-purpose flour, sifted
½ teaspoon salt
1 (1 pound) package orange slice candy, cut into small pieces
8 ounces pitted dates, chopped
2 cups walnuts or pecans, chopped
3¼ or 1 can coconut
2 cups sugar
1 cup butter or margarine
4 eggs
1 teaspoon baking soda
½ cup buttermilk
1 cup orange juice
2 cups powdered sugar

Sift flour and salt. Combine orange slices, dates, nuts, and coconut. Take ½ cup flour and cut up candy in it. Mix the butter and gradually add sugar. Beat well. Add eggs one at a time. Combine 1 teaspoon baking soda and ½ cup buttermilk. Add this mixture alternately with flour mixture, blending well. Add orange slices, nuts and coconut. Pour into a greased and floured pan. Bake at 300° for 1 hour and 45 minutes. I place a coffee can of water in the oven when I bake this. Remove from oven. Combine orange juice and powdered sugar. Mix well and pour over hot cake. Cool, refrigerate overnight before removing from pan.

Dump Cake

2 cans cherry pie filling
1 large can crushed pineapple in heavy syrup
½ cup sugar
1 box yellow cake mix
2 sticks butter or margarine
1 cup pecans

Butter a 9x13-inch baking pan. Spread 2 cans of cherry pie filling in the pan. Spread 1 can crushed pineapple with juice over pie filling. Sprinkle sugar over pineapple. Spread dry yellow cake mix over sugar. Dot 2 sticks of butter over top of mix, then with sprinkle pecans. Bake in a 350° oven for 45 minutes.

Cream Cheese Pound Cake

1½ cups butter, softened
1 (8 ounce) package cream cheese, softened
3 cups sugar
6 large eggs
3 cups all purpose flour
⅛ teaspoon salt
1 tablespoon vanilla extract

Beat butter and cream cheese at medium speed with an electric mixer until creamy. Gradually add sugar, beating until light and fluffy. Add eggs, one at a time, beating just until blended after each addition. Combine flour and salt; gradually add to butter mixture, beating at a low speed just until blended. Stir in vanilla. Spoon batter into a greased and floured 10-inch tube pan. Bake at 300° for 1 hour and 45 minutes or until a long wooden pick inserted in center comes out clean. Cool in a pan on a wire rack for 15 minutes; remove from pan, and let cool completely on wire rack.

Blueberry Cobbler

3½ cups fresh blueberries or 1 bag frozen blueberries
1 tablespoon cornstarch
2 tablespoon lemon juice
1 cup all-purpose flour
¾ cup granulated sugar
1 teaspoon baking powder
¼ teaspoon salt
½ cup milk
3 tablespoon butter, melted
¾ cup boiling water

Heat oven to 350°. Spread blueberries in an ungreased 8- or 9-inch square baking dish. Sprinkle with cornstarch; drizzle with lemon juice, set aside.

In a medium bowl, combine flour, ½ cup of sugar, baking powder and salt. Add milk and butter, stir just until combined (not smooth). Drop 9 mounds of dough onto blueberries. Pour boiling water over dough and fruit. Sprinkle with remaining ¼ cup of sugar. Bake until dough is golden brown and blueberries are bubbly, 45-50 minutes. Serve warm or at room temperature.

Apple Crisp (No sugar added)

Yields 10 servings

7 medium Granny Smith apples
2 teaspoons ground cinnamon
1 cup Splenda

Topping:
2 cups oats
¼ cup flour
¼ cup Splenda
½ cup margarine, melted

Preheat oven to 350°. Place in greased 9x13-inch baking dish. Add cinnamon and sweetener. Stir until the cinnamon covers all the apples. In a separate bowl, mix topping ingredients. Sprinkle over apple mixture. Bake for 40 minutes.

Traditional Apple Dumplings

3 cups all-purpose flour
2 teaspoons baking powder
1 teaspoon salt
1 cup shortening
¾ cup milk
3 large Granny Smith, Winesap, or other cooking apples
2 tablespoons butter or margarine
1 tablespoon sugar
1½ teaspoons ground cinnamon
1½ cups sugar
1 cup orange juice
½ cup water
1 tablespoon butter or margarine
¼ teaspoon ground cinnamon
¼ teaspoon ground nutmeg

Combine flour, baking powder, and salt; cut in shortening with a pastry blender until mixture resembles coarse meal. Gradually add milk, stirring with a fork until dry ingredients are moistened. Shape into a ball. Roll pastry to ¼-inch thickness on a lightly floured surface, shaping into a 21x14-inch rectangle. Cut pastry into 6 (7-inch) squares with a fluted pastry wheel.

Peel and core apples; cut in half crosswise. Place one apple half, cut side down, on each pastry square; dot each apple half with 1 teaspoon butter. Sprinkle each with ½ teaspoon sugar and ¼ teaspoon cinnamon. Moisten edges of each pastry square with water; bring corners to the center, pressing edges to seal. Place dumplings in a lightly greased 13x9x2-inch baking dish. Bake at 375° for 35 minutes or until apples are tender and pastry is lightly browned.

Combine 1½ cups sugar, orange juice, water, 1 tablespoon butter, ¼ teaspoon cinnamon, and nutmeg in a medium saucepan. Bring to a boil; reduce heat, and simmer, uncovered, 4 minutes or until butter melts and sugar dissolves, stirring occasionally. Pour syrup over dumplings, and serve immediately.

Blackberry Dumplings

Yields 6 servings

1 quart frozen blackberries
1 cup sugar
½ teaspoon lemon extract
¾ teaspoon salt, divided
1½ cups all-purpose flour
2 teaspoons baking powder
1 tablespoon sugar
¼ teaspoon ground nutmeg
⅔ cup milk
Whipped cream (optional)

Bring first 3 ingredients and ¼ teaspoon salt to a boil in a large ovenproof casserole dish; reduce heat, and simmer 5 minutes.

Combine remaining ½ teaspoon salt, flour, baking powder, 1 tablespoon sugar, and nutmeg in a medium bowl; stir in milk just until blended (dough will be thick). Drop dough by tablespoons onto hot blackberry mixture. Bake at 400° for 35 minutes or until golden. Serve with whipped cream, if desired.

Peach Cobbler

2½ pounds fresh peaches
½ cup water
2 tablespoons cornstarch
1 cup flour
1½ teaspoons baking powder
¼ cup butter
1 egg
¾ cup sugar
½ teaspoon nutmeg
Butter
2 tablespoons sugar
¼ teaspoon salt
¼ cup milk

Remove pits form peaches and slice. Place peach slices in a 9-inch square pan, set aside. In pan combine ¾ cup sugar, water, nutmeg, and cornstarch. Mix well, bring to a boil and boil 1 minute. Pour syrup over peaches in pan.

Dot with butter. Combine flour, 2 tablespoons sugar, baking powder and salt. Cut in ¼ cup butter until mixture resembles coarse crumbs. Add milk and egg, stirring just until moistened. Drop cobbler dough by spoonfuls over sliced peaches. Bake in 425° oven for about 20 minutes or until golden brown.

Favorite Layer Bars

Yields 3 dozen

1½ cups graham cracker crumbs
¼ cup sugar
⅓ cup margarine, melted
1 (8 ounce) package Philadelphia cream cheese, softened
½ cup sugar
1 egg
¾ cup flaked coconut
¾ cup chopped nuts
1 (6 ounce) package semi-sweet chocolate chips

Combine crumbs, sugar and margarine, press onto bottom of 13x9-inch baking pan. Bake at 350º for 5 minutes.

Combine cream cheese, sugar and egg, mixing until well blended. Spread over crust. Sprinkle with remaining ingredients; press lightly into surface. Bake at 350º for 25-30 minutes or until lightly browned. Cool, cut into bars.

Diabetic Brownies

Yields 16 squares

2 cups fine graham crackers crumbs (about 24 crackers)
½ cup chopped walnuts
3 ounces semi-sweet chocolate pieces
1½ teaspoons Sweet'N Low
1 cup skim milk
¼ teaspoon salt

Preheat oven to 350º. Place all ingredients in a bowl and stir until blended well. Put into a greased and floured 8x8x2-inch pan. Bake 30 minutes. Cut into squares while warm.

Mint Bars

Yields 3 dozen

½ cup butter (no substitutes)
⅓ cup baking cocoa
¼ cup sugar
1 egg, beaten
1¾ cups graham cracker crumbs
¾ cup flaked coconut
½ cup finely chopped walnuts

Filling:
⅓ cup butter, softened
2 cups confectioners' sugar
3 tablespoons milk
1 teaspoon peppermint extract
Green food coloring, optional

Topping:
Semi-sweet chocolate chips
2 tablespoons butter

In a heavy saucepan, heat the butter, cocoa and sugar over low heat until sugar is dissolved, stirring often. Remove from the heat. Stir a small amount of hot mixture into egg; return all to the pan. Cook and stir until mixture coats a metal spoon and reaches 160°. Remove from the heat. Stir in the cracker crumbs, coconut, and walnuts. Press into a buttered 9-inch square pan; set aside. For filling, in a small mixing bowl, beat butter, confectioners' sugar, milk, and extract until smooth. Tint with food coloring if desired. Spread evenly over bottom layer; set aside. For topping, in a heavy saucepan, melt chocolate chips and butter over low heat until blended and smooth, stirring often. Remove from heat. Cool to room temperature, about 10 minutes. Spread over filling. Cover and refrigerate until set, about 1 hour. Cut into bars. Store in the refrigerator.

Double Fudge Chocolate Brownies

1 package Duncan Hines Double Chocolate Brownie mix
2 medium eggs
⅓ cup water
¼ cup vegetable oil
½ cup chopped pecans

Topping:
1 (8 ounce) package Philadelphia cream cheese
2 medium eggs
1 pound powdered sugar
1 teaspoon vanilla extract

Preheat oven to 350º. With an electric mixer, beat eggs, add water, and oil. Fold in brownie mix and pecans. Mix by hand well enough to blend. Grease bottom of 9x13x2-inch pan; pour brownie mix into greased pan.

Soften the cream cheese, add eggs, and vanilla extract, and blend well with electric mixer. Add powdered sugar. Mix well. Pour over top of brownie mix, spread evenly. If you would like, sprinkle top lightly with finely ground pecans. Bake 45 minutes. Cool, cut into desired serving size and serve.

Very Chocolate Brownies

Yields 3 dozen

4 squares (1 ounce each) unsweetened chocolate
¾ cup butter (no substitutes)
2 cups sugar
3 eggs
1 teaspoon vanilla extract
1 cup all-purpose flour
1 cup coarsely chopped walnuts

Topping:
1 cup semi-sweet chocolate chips
¼ cup water
2 tablespoons butter (no substitutes)
1 cup whipping cream, whipped

In a microwave or double boiler, melt chocolate and butter; cool for 10 minutes. Add sugar; mix well. Stir in eggs and vanilla. Add flour; mix well.

Stir in the walnuts. Line a 13x 9x2-inch baking pan with foil and grease the foil. Pour batter into pan. Bake at 350º for 25-30 minutes or until a toothpick inserted near the center comes out with moist crumbs (do not overbake). Cool completely. For topping, melt chocolate chips, water and butter in a microwave or double boiler; stir until smooth. Cool to room temperature. Fold in whipped cream. Spread over brownies. Chill before cutting. Store leftovers in the refrigerator.

Chunky Blonde Brownies

Yields 2 dozen

½ cup butter or margarine, softened
¾ cup sugar
¾ cup packed brown sugar
2 eggs
2 teaspoons vanilla extract
1½ cups all-purpose flour
1 teaspoon baking powder
½ teaspoon salt
1 cup vanilla chips
1 cup semi-sweet chocolate chunks
1 jar (3½ ounces) macadamia nuts or ¾ cup blanched almonds, chopped, divided

In a mixing bowl, cream butter and sugars. Add the eggs and vanilla; mix well. Combine flour, baking powder and salt; add to creamed mixture and mix well. Stir in vanilla chips, chocolate chunks, and ½ cup nuts. Spoon into greased 13x9x2-inch baking pan; spread to evenly cover bottom of pan. Sprinkle with remaining nuts. Bake at 350º for 25-30 minutes or until golden brown. Cool on a wire rack.

Cappuccino Brownies

Yields 16 bars

½ cup butter or margarine
3 ounces unsweetened chocolate, cut up
1 cup granulated sugar
2 eggs
1 teaspoon vanilla
⅔ cup all-purpose flour
¼ teaspoon baking soda
1 teaspoon instant coffee crystals
1 tablespoon whipping cream
1 cup sifted powdered sugar
2 tablespoons butter or margarine
Chocolate frosting

Melt ½ cup butter or margarine and unsweetened chocolate in a medium saucepan over low heat; stirring constantly. Remove from heat; cool slightly. Stir in granulated sugar. Add eggs, one at a time, beating with wooden spoon just until combined. Stir in vanilla.

Stir together flour and baking soda in a small bowl. Add flour mixture to chocolate mixture and stir just until combined. Spread batter in a greased 8x8x2-inch baking pan. Bake in a 350° oven for 30 minutes.

Meanwhile, for topping, dissolve coffee crystals in whipping cream. Beat together powdered sugar and the 2 tablespoons butter or margarine in a small mixing bowl with an electric mixer on medium speed. Add whipping cream to mixture and beat until creamy. If necessary, add a little additional whipping cream until mixture is spreading consistency. Spread over the warm brownies. Chill about 1 hour or until topping is set. Carefully spread Chocolate Frosting over brownies. Chill until frosting is set. Cut into bars.

Chocolate Frosting

1 cup semisweet chocolate pieces
⅓ cup whipping cream

Combine 1 cup semisweet choclate pieces and ⅓ cup whipping cream in small pan. Stir over low heat until chocolate is melted and mixture begins to thicken.

Best Oatmeal Cookies

Yields about 4½ dozen

1¼ cups (2½ sticks) margarine, softened
¾ cup firmly packed brown sugar
½ cup granulated sugar
1 egg
1 teaspoon vanilla
1½ cups all-purpose flour
1 teaspoon baking soda
½ teaspoon baking salt (optional)
1 teaspoon ground cinnamon
¼ teaspoon ground nutmeg
3 cups Quaker Oats (quick or old fashioned, uncooked)

Heat oven to 375º. Beat margarine and sugars until creamy. Beat in egg and vanilla. Add combined flour, baking soda, salt, and spices; mix well. Stir in oats. Drop by rounded tablespoonsful onto ungreased cookie sheet. Bake 8-9 mintues for a chewy cookie, 10-11 minutes for a crisp cookie. Cool 1 minute on cookie sheet; remove to wire rack.

No-Bake Orange Coconut Balls

1 stick butter or margarine
16-ounce box powdered sugar
6-ounce can orange juice concentrate, thawed
12-ounce box vanilla wafers, finely crushed
7-ounce package sweetened coconut

Cream butter and sugar in a large bowl, mixing well. Add juice and wafers and mix again. Pinch off small amounts and roll into balls the size of a dime. Roll the balls in the coconut and place in covered container. Refrigerate until ready to serve. This recipe freezes well.

Truffle Cookies

Yields 54-60 cookies

3 (4 ounce) bars sweet baking chocolate, chopped
2 tablespoons butter
1 teaspoon instant coffee grandules
3 eggs
1¼ cups granulated sugar
1 teaspoon vanilla
1 cup chopped pecans
6 tablespoons all-purpose flour
1 teaspoon ground cinnamon
½ teaspoon baking powder
¼ teaspoon salt
Nonstick spray coating
Pecan halves (optional)

In a small saucepan, heat and stir chocolate and shortening over very low heat until chocolate begins to melt. Remove from heat. Add coffee. Stir until smooth. Cool.

Beat eggs and sugar with an electric mixer on medium to high speed until light and lemon colored (3 or 4 minutes). Beat in chocolate mixture and vanilla. On low speed beat in pecans, flour, cinnamon, baking powder, and salt until combined.

Spray cookie sheets with nonstick coating. Drop teaspoonful of dough 2 inches apart on cookie sheets. Place a pecan half atop each cookie, if desired. Bake in a 350° oven for 8-10 minutes or until just set on surface (do not overbake). Cool for 1 to 2 minutes; transfer to racks. Cool completely.

Dixie Peanut Brittle

2 cups sugar
1 cup light corn syrup
½ cup water
½ teaspoon salt
3 cups raw, shelled peanuts, skins on
2 tablespoons butter
2 teaspoons baking soda

Line a baking sheet with foil and coat it with butter. Heat sugar, syrup, water, and salt in a heavy saucepan to a rolling boil, stirring constantly. Add peanuts. Reduce heat to medium and continue to stir. Cook to hard crack stage (293º). Turn off the heat, and add the butter and baking soda. Beat rapidly until well mixed, then pour onto the buttered baking sheet, spreading the mixture to ¼-inch thickness. Allow candy to cool completely; break into pieces and store in an airtight container.

Melting Moments

Yields 3 dozen cookies

1 cup unsifted flour
½ cup cornstarch
½ cup confectioners' sugar
¾ cup margarine
1 teaspoon vanilla or almond flavoring

Stir together flour, cornstarch, and sugar. In a large bowl with mixer at medium speed, beat margarine until smooth. Add flour mixture and flavoring; beat until well blended. Refrigerate for 1 hour. Shape into 1-inch balls. Place 1½ inches apart on ungreased cookie sheet; flatten with fingers or bottom of glass. Bake in 375° oven for 10-12 minutes. Cool.

This is my favorite cookie!

Sand Tarts

3 cups flour
3 tablespoons powdered sugar
½ pound of butter
1 cup pecans

Soften butter, add flour and sugar. Add nuts and vanilla to taste. Roll with hands and shape in small crescents. Bake at 325° until golden brown. Roll in powdered sugar while warm.

Sugarless Cookies

1 cup flour
1½ teaspoons cinnamon
1 teaspoon soda
½ teaspoon salt
¼ teaspoon nutmeg
1 teaspoon clove
1 teaspoon allspice
1 cup quick oats
1 cup raisins
1 cup unsweetened applesauce
½ cup oil
2 eggs
1 teaspoon vanilla
½ cup nuts

Mix dry ingredients and add remaining ingredients to moisten. Dough will be thin. Drop by teaspoonfuls onto cookie sheet. Bake at 375° for 12 minutes.

Peanut Butter Snowballs

Yields 2 dozen

1 cup confectioners' sugar
½ cup creamy peanut butter
3 tablespoons butter, softened
1 pound white candy coating

In a mixing bowl, combine sugar, peanut butter and butter; mix well. Shape into 1-inch balls and place on waxed paper-lined baking sheet. Chill for 30 minutes or until firm.

Meanwhile, melt the candy coating in a double boiler or microwave-safe bowl. Dip balls and place on waxed paper to harden.

Peanut Butter Blossoms

Yields 4 dozen cookies

48 Hershey's Kisses
½ cup shortening
¾ cup creamy peanut butter
⅓ cup granulated sugar
⅓ cup packed light brown sugar
1 egg
2 tablespoons milk
1 teaspoon vanilla extract
1½ cups all-purpose flour
1 teaspoon baking soda
½ teaspoon salt
Granulated sugar

Heat oven to 375°. Remove foil from Hershey's Kisses.

Beat shortening and peanut butter in large bowl until well blended. Add ⅓ cup granulated sugar and brown sugar; beat well. Stir together flour, baking soda and salt; gradually beat into peanut butter mixture.

Shape dough into 1-inch balls. Roll in granulated sugar; place on ungreased cookie sheet.

Bake 8-10 minutes or until lightly browned. Immediately press a chocolate into center of each cookie; cookie will crack around edges. Remove from cookie sheet to wire rack and allow to cool completely.

Tea Time Tassies

Yields 2 dozen

¾ cup firmly packed light brown sugar
¾ cup chopped pecans
1 egg
1 tablespoon butter or margarine, softened
1 teaspoon vanilla extract
Dash of salt
Tart shells
Powdered sugar (optional)

Combine first 6 ingredients. Spoon mixture into tart shells, filling ¾ full. Bake at 350° for 20 minutes or until brown. Dust with powdered sugar before serving, if desired.

Tart Shell

Yields 2 dozen

1 cup all-purpose flour
1 (3 ounce) package cream cheese, softened
½ cup plus 3 tablespoons butter, softened

Combine all ingredients; stir until well blended. Shape dough into 24 balls; chill. Place in greased 1¾-inch tart pans, shaping each ball into a shell.

Peanut Butter Oat Bars

Yields 39 bars

2 cups quick oats
1½ cups unsifted flour
1 teaspoon baking powder
¼ teaspoon salt
⅔ cup chunky peanut butter
2 tablespoons butter or margarine
1 cup sugar
⅓ cup dark corn syrup
2 eggs
1 teaspoon vanilla
2 cups raisins

Spread oats in a 15½x10½x-inch jelly-roll pan. Bake them in a 400° oven, stirring occasionally, 8-10 minutes or until lightly toasted. Cool. Grease a 13x9x2-inch pan. In a small bowl, stir together the flour, baking powder, and salt. In a larger bowl with a mixer at medium speed, beat the peanut butter and butter or margarine until well mixed. Beat in the sugar, corn syrup, eggs, and vanilla until well blended, then beat in flour mixture until well mixed. With a wooden spoon, stir in the oats and raisins and spread evenly in a prepared pan. Bake in a 350° oven about 25 minutes, or until a cake tester in the center comes out clean. Cool on a rack and cut into 3 x 1-inch bars.

Quick Cherry Dessert

1 cup butter or margarine
1½ cup granulated sugar
4 eggs
1 teaspoon almond extract
2 cups all-purpose flour
2 teaspoons baking powder
1 (21 ounce) can cherry pie filling
Whipped cream, optional
Powdered sugar to dust over top, optional

In a large mixing bowl, cream together the butter and sugar. Add the eggs. Beat until light and fluffy. Add the almond extract. Stir in the flour and baking powder. Mix until smooth. Butter a 13x9-inch cake pan. Turn the mixture into the pan. Spoon the pie filling into the cake.

Bake at 350° for 45-50 minutes or until golden and cake tests done. Filling will sink into the cake while baking.

Place bottom side up on a serving plate. Dust with powdered sugar, if used. Spoon slightly sweetened whipped cream over each serving, if desired. This is great served warm.

Note: For blueberry dessert, substitute blueberry filling for the cherry filling.

Hot Cranberry Bake

4 cups peeled chopped cooking apples
2 cups fresh cranberries
1½ teaspoons lemon juice
1 cup sugar
1⅓ cups quick-cooking oats, uncooked
Pinch of salt
1 cup chopped walnuts
⅓ cup firmly packed brown sugar
½ cup butter or margarine, melted
Vanilla ice cream

Layer apples and cranberries in a lightly greased 2-quart baking dish. Sprinkle with lemon juice; spoon sugar over fruit, set aside.

Combine oats and next 3 ingredients; stir just until dry ingredients are moistened and mixture is crumbly. Sprinkle over fruit. Bake uncovered, at 325° for 1 hour. Serve dessert warm with vanilla ice cream.

Peach Freeze

Yields 12 servings

2 cups crushed macaroon cookies
2 cups mashed fresh peaches (4-5 peaches)
1 cup sugar
1 cup whipping cream (½ pint)

Put 1 cup crumbs on bottom of 8x12-inch dish. Combine peaches and sugar. Whip cream and fold in peaches and spoon over crumbs. Top with remaining crumbs. Freeze and cut into squares.

Pumpkin Roll with Cream Cheese Filling

Yields 10 servings

Cake:
Powdered sugar
Cream cheese
¾ cup all-purpose flour
½ teaspoon baking powder
½ teaspoon baking soda
½ teaspoon ground cinnamon
½ teaspoon ground cloves
¼ teaspoon salt
3 large eggs
1 cup granulated sugar
⅔ cup pure pumpkin
1 cup chopped walnuts

Filling:
1 (8 ounce) package cream cheese, softened
1 cup sifted powdered sugar
6 tablespoons butter or oleo
1 teaspoon vanilla extract
Powdered sugar

Preheat oven 375°. Grease 15x10-inch jelly-roll pan; line with wax paper. Grease and flour paper. Sprinkle towel with powdered sugar. Combine flour, baking powder, baking soda, cinnamon, cloves, and salt in a small bowl. Beat eggs and sugar in large mixer bowl until thick. Beat in pumpkin. Stir in flour mixture. Spread evenly into prepared pan. Sprinkle with nuts, if desired.

Bake for 13-15 minutes or until top of cake springs back when touched. Immediately loosen and turn cake onto prepared towel. Carefully peel off paper. Roll up cake and towel together, starting with the narrow end. Cool on wire rack.

Beat cream cheese, powdered sugar, butter, and vanilla extract in a small mixing bowl until smooth. Carefully unroll cake; remove towel. Spread cream cheese mixture over cake. Re-roll cake. Wrap in plastic wrap and refrigerate at least one hour. Sprinkle with powdered sugar before serving, if desired.

Rhubarb Crunch

2 cups flour
1½ cup quick oats
1 cup melted oleo or butter
2 teaspoons cinnamon
5 cup raw rhubarb, diced
1½ cup sugar
2 tablespoons cornstarch
1 cup water
1 teaspoon vanilla flavoring

Mix first 5 ingredients until crumbly. Press ½ of this mixture into a greased 9x13 pan. Cover with rhubarb. Cook sugar, cornstarch and water until thick and clear; remove from heat. Add vanilla and pour syrup over rhubarb. Sprinkle rest of crumbly mixture over top and pat lightly. Bake in a 350° oven for 45-55 minutes.

Sweet Potato Cobbler

2 cups sweet potatoes, sliced
1 cup sugar
2 cups water
Pie dough
2 tablespoons sugar

Combine potatoes, 1 cup sugar, salt, and water in a saucepan; boil 5 minutes. Cover bottom and sides of deep casserole dish with pie dough. Pour potato mixture over pie dough. Cut up small strips of the pie dough (approximately 1 cup). Drop into potato mixture. Cut butter over mixture. Cover potato mixture with large pie; place dots of butter over top of crust. Sprinkle top of crust with sugar. Bake at 350° for 30 minutes.

Tips for Better Pies

1. When using refrigerated pie crusts, fold crusts in half before placing in pie plate.
2. Bring a small amount of excess crust over outside rim of pie plate to lock it in place while it bakes. Excess crust can be chipped away with a knife blade after baking.
3. If your pie crust tears, dampen the torn edges, and gently press together.
4. Pipe a whipped cream edge lattice design by alternating horizontal and vertical rows on top of the pies.
5. Drain berries and other fruit on layers of paper towels before placing them on the pie. This prevents excess liquid and discoloration of custard fillings.
6. Use a wooden pick to place chocolate curls on top of pie; warm fingers can melt or crush the curls.
7. You can wrap an unbaked homemade crust and store it in the freezer for up to two months.
8. Place wax paper on surface of hot custard fillings before placing in refrigerator to chill. Paper will prevent a film from forming on top of custard.

Blackberry Pie

"The Wild Flavor"

Pastry for a double crust pie
4 cups ripe blackberries
1 cup sugar
3 tablespoons tapioca
2 tablespoons butter
Milk

Fill pastry-lined pan with blackberries mixed with sugar and tapioca. Dot top with butter. Cover berries with top crust, cutting a vent in the center to let the steam escape. Trim and crimp edges of crust, brush with milk then sprinkle with additional sugar. Bake in a 400° oven for 10 minutes, then continue baking at 350° for about 40 minutes or until top crust is browned and berry juices thicken and bubble. Serve warm.

Banana Cream Pie

Nut Crust:
2 cups pecans
1 cup butter, softened
3 cups flour
1 egg, beaten
½ cup sugar

Chocolate Layer:
1 cup chocolate chips
1 stick unsalted butter
1 tablespoon light corn syrup
1 teaspoon vanilla

Banana Custard:
1 cup milk
4 egg yolks
1 cup sugar
5 tablespoons flour
3 tablespoons unsalted butter
1 tablespoon rum or 1 teaspoon vanilla
2 bananas
Juice of ½ lemon
2 cups heavy cream
Chopped pecans, optional

Crust: Chop pecans very fine, preferably in a food processor fitted with a metal blade. Place in bowl with other crust ingredients and mix until well blended. Divide in half and press into the bottom of 2 pie pans. Chill 30 minutes. Bake the pie crusts for 25 minutes at 350°. Cool completely.

Chocolate Layer: Melt chocolate with butter and corn syrup in the top boiler over hot, but not boiling water. Stir frequently. Remove from heat and cool, then stir in vanilla. Divide between cooked pie crusts and spread evenly.

Filling: Heat milk in a medium-size saucepan over medium heat to scald. Beat the egg yolks and gradually add sugar. Then beat in flour. Gradually stir in hot milk. Transfer to a medium saucepan and cook, stirring constantly over medium-high heat (use a wisk). The mixture will lump as it begins to thicken. Bring the mixture to a boil and boil 1 minute, stirring constantly. Remove the pan from heat and continue to stir until the mixture is smooth. Then beat in butter, vanilla or optional rum. Cool to room temperature.

Peel the bananas, slice very thin and toss with lemon juice. Whip 1 cup of the cream until it is firm but not stiff. Mix about ¼ of the cream into the cooled egg mixture to lighten it, then fold the remaining cream and bananas into egg mixture. Fill the pastry shells with banana cream and smooth to even. Beat remaining cream until stiff. Spoon around the edge of the pies and sprinkle with chopped pecans, if desired.

Coconut Cream Pie

1 cup sugar
4 tablespoons all-purpose flour
1 tablespoon butter
3 egg yolks*
½ teaspoon vanilla
1½ cups milk
¼ cup evaporated milk

Cook mixture in saucepan until thick. Add coconut and pour in 9-inch baked pie shell. Meringue: Break three egg whites and combine with ⅛ teaspoon cream of tartar and ⅛ teaspoon vanilla. Beat until fluffy, then add ⅛ cup sugar. Beat until mixture stands up in peaks then spread over pie and top with coconut. Brown in oven
*Save whites for meringue

Diabetic Coconut Pie

2 eggs, well beaten
4 packages artificial sweetener
4 tablespoons melted butter
1¾ cup sweet milk
1 cup coconut

Mix all ingredients and pour into unbaked pie shell. Bake at 350° for 45 to 60 minutes.

Mom's Custard Pie

1 unbaked pastry shell
4 eggs
½ cup sugar
¼ teaspoon salt
1 teaspoon vanilla extract
2½ cups milk
¼ teaspoon ground nutmeg

Line unpricked pastry shell with a double thickness of heavy-duty foil. Bake at 450° for 8 minutes. Remove foil; bake 5 minutes longer. Remove from the oven and set aside. Separate one egg; set the white aside. In a mixing bowl, beat the yolk and remaining eggs just until combined. Blend in sugar, salt and vanilla. Stir in milk. Beat reserved egg white until stiff peaks form; fold into egg mixture. Carefully pour into crust. Cover edges of pie with foil. Bake at 350° for 25 minutes. Remove foil; bake 15-20 minutes longer or until a knife inserted near the center comes out clean. Cool on a wire rack. Sprinkle with nutmeg. Store in the refrigerator.

Tom's Holiday Pie

1½ cup sugar
1½ heaping teaspoons cornstarch
1 teaspoon cinnamon
⅛ teaspoon nutmeg
Pinch of salt
3 teaspoons vinegar
½ stick butter, beaten well
1 teaspoon vanilla
1 cup chopped pecans
1 cup raisins

Pre-heat oven to 325°. Start with the three well-beaten eggs and add the following ingredients in the order listed, mixing well after each. Pour mixture into an unbaked 9-inch pie crust. Bake 45 minutes to an hour, or until pie "sets" and is light golden brown. Cool before serving.

Lemon Meringue Pie

1 cup sugar
¼ cup cornstarch
3 egg yolks, slightly beaten
Grated peel of one lemon
¼ cup lemon juice
1 tablespoon butter or margarine
1 baked pie crust
3 egg whites
⅓ cup sugar

Preheat oven to 350°. In medium saucepan combine 1 cup sugar and cornstarch. Stir in water until smooth. Stir in egg yolks.

Stirring constantly, bring to a boil over medium heat; boil 1 minute. Remove from heat. Stir in lemon peel, juice and butter. Spoon hot filling into pie crust.

In a small mixing bowl, beat egg whites at high speed until foamy. Gradually beat in remaining ⅓ cups of sugar; continue beating until stiff peaks form. Spread meringue evenly over hot filling, sealing to crust.

Bake 15-20 minutes or until golden brown. Cool on wire rack; refrigerate.

Lemon Chiffon Pie

1 baked pie crust
½ cup sugar
1 envelope unflavored gelatin
⅔ cup water
⅓ cup lemon juice
4 eggs
1 tablespoon grated lemon rind
½ teaspoon cream of tartar
½ cups sugar

In a microwave dish combine sugar, gelatin, and water. Add lemon juice, beaten egg yolks. Cook on high for approximately 4 minutes. Stir two or three times during cooking. Remove from microwave, add lemon rind and cool.

Make a meringue of the egg whites, cream of tartar, and sugar. When stiff, fold into cooked gelatin custard. Pile into a baked pie crust or graham cracker crust. Chill well. Serve with a dollop of whipped cream and a mint sprig.

Fresh Peach Pie

1 cup sugar
⅓ cup butter
⅓ cup flour
1 egg
⅓ cup flour
1 teaspoon pure almond extract
Fresh, sliced peaches
Pie crust

Place peaches in pie crust. Cream first 4 ingredients, then beat in flour and almond extract. Spread over peaches. Bake approximately 1 hour at 350°

Chocolate Chunk Pecan Pie

1 unbaked 9-inch deep-dish pie shell
3 large eggs
1 cup light corn syrup
½ cup granulated sugar
¼ cup butter or margarine, melted
1 teaspoon vanilla extract
1 cup pecan halves, coarsely chopped
¾ cup semi-sweet chocolate chunks

Preheat oven to 350°. Combine eggs, corn syrup, sugar, butter, and vanilla extract in medium bowl with a wire whisk. Stir in pecans. Sprinkle chunks over bottom of crust. Pour pecan mixture into pie shell.

Bake for 50-55 minutes or until knife inserted 2 inches from center comes out with little bits of filing attached. If browning too quickly, cover with foil. Cool on wire rack for 2 hours; refrigerate until serving time.

Strawberry Pie

1 warm 9-inch baked pie shell
2 tablespoons melted butter
2 tablespoons sugar
About 3 dozen whole, perfect strawberries, washed and hulled
½ cup water
1 cup sugar
2½ tablespoons cornstarch
1 tablespoon butter

While pie crust is still warm, sprinkle with melted butter and the 2 tablespoons of sugar. Set aside. When cool, place strawberries, tips up, inside pie crust.

In a medium saucepan, combine the remaining ingredients and bring to a gentle simmer. Cook over medium heat about 5 minutes, until thick and clear.

Pour glaze over tips of berries. Chill pie. Slice into wedges and serve with whipped cream or ice cream.

Note: a drop of red food coloring may be added to glaze if red color is faint.

Lemon Pudding

2 eggs, separated
¼ cup flour
¼ teaspoon salt
1½ tablespoons lemon juice
1 tablespoon grated lemon rind
1 cup sugar
1 cup milk

Sift together flour, sugar, and salt, add lemon juice and grated rind. Beat egg yolks until light, then add milk. Pour this mixture slowly into flour mixture. Fold in egg whites that are beaten stiff. Pour into greased Pyrex baking dish and set in pan with about 1 inch of water. Bake at 350° for 35 minutes.

Rice Pudding

3 cups cooked rice
3 cups milk
½ cup sugar
Dash of salt
2 eggs, beaten
2 tablespoons butter
1 teaspoon vanilla

In a large saucepan, combine rice, milk, sugar, butter, and salt. Cook over medium heat until thick and creamy. Stir often. Add a small amount of the mixture to the eggs, mixing well. Stir into remaining hot mixture. Cook 2 minutes, stirring constantly. Remove from heat and stir in vanilla. You may also add up to 1 cup chopped nuts, chopped fruit, raisins, candied fruit—but this is simply delicious plain with a sprinkle of nutmeg or cinnamon.

No-Fail Skillet Rice Custard

Yields 8 servings
1 cup cooked Riceland Plump & Tender Medium Grain Rice
5 eggs
3½ cups milk
¾ cup sugar
1 teaspoon vanilla extract
¼ teaspoon salt

About 2 hours before serving, in a medium mixing bowl with wire whisk, beat eggs, milk, sugar, vanilla, and salt until well blended. Fold in cooked rice. Pour mixture into 8 (6 ounce) custard cups. Place cups in a large electric skillet; pour water into skillet to come halfway up sides of cups. Over medium heat (350°), heat water just to boiling. Cover skillet and turn off heat; let custard stand in covered skillet 15-20 minutes. Remove custard cups from skillet. Sprinkle with nutmeg, if desired. Chill in refrigerator until ready to serve.

Fruit 'N Rice Pudding

Yields 4 servings

1½ cups milk
⅔ cup quick-cooking rice
¼ cup sugar
2 tablespoons margarine or butter
2 eggs
¼ cup light raisins, dried cherries, or snipped dried apricots
½ teaspoon vanilla
¼ teaspoon ground cinnamon, ginger, or cardamom
1½ cups of water
Milk or light cream (optional)

In a 1-quart microwave-safe casserole combine the milk, uncooked quick-cooking rice, sugar, and margarine or butter. Cook, uncovered on 100% power (high) for 3 to 5 minutes or just to boiling, stirring once to dissolve the sugar.

In a small mixing bowl beat the eggs with a fork. Gradually stir 1 cup of the hot mixture into the beaten eggs. Return all of the mixture into the casserole. Stir in the fruit, vanilla, and cinnamon, ginger, or cardamom. Set mixture aside.

Meanwhile in a 4-cup measure heat water, uncovered, on high for 3 to 5 minutes or until boiling. Place the filled casserole in an 8x8x2-inch microwave-safe baking dish. Pour the boiling water into the baking dish around the casserole (should be a depth of about 1 inch).

Cook, uncovered, on 50% power (medium) for 4 minutes; stir. Continue cooking for 4 to 6 minutes or until pudding tests done (a knife inserted 1 inch from the edge comes out clean). The top may still appear wet. Cover the pudding surface with plastic wrap or waxed paper; let stand on a wire rack for 15 minutes. If desired, serve warm or chilled with milk or light cream. Sprinkle with additional cinnamon if desired.

Jiffy Banana Pudding

2 boxes vanilla instant pudding mix
3 cups milk
1 large container whipped topping
1 (8 ounce) container sour cream
2 boxes vanilla wafers
6 large bananas

Fold, don't beat, the first four ingredients together. Layer vanilla wafers, bananas, and pudding mixture. Sprinkle crumbled wafers on top. This luscious banana pudding only takes an instant to make. It's a good thing that it goes just as fast. So eat up and enjoy.

Microwave Banana Pudding

Yields 10-12 servings

3½ tablespoons flour
1½ cups sugar
¼ teaspoon salt
3 cups milk
3 eggs, separated
1 teaspoon vanilla
1 (12 ounce) box vanilla wafers
6 medium bananas
⅓ cup sugar

Combine first four ingredients in an 8-cup microwavable bowl, and stir well. Add egg yolks and vanilla, and beat well. Cook on high for 4 minutes and stir well. Then cook 3 to 4 minutes more until thickened and stir well.

Layer ⅓ box of vanilla wafers in a 9x9 Pyrex dish, slice 2 bananas over them and pour ⅓ of the custard over bananas. Repeat layer twice. Beat egg whites and remaining sugar until stiff and firm. Spread meringue over filling, sealing edges well. Bake in preheated 400° oven for 10 to 12 minute or until browned.

Bread Pudding with Warm Praline Sauce

½ cup of packed golden brown sugar
¼ light corn syrup
2 tablespoons unsalted butter
2 tablespoons Brandy
2 cinnamon sticks
1 tablespoon rum
1½ teaspoons vanilla extract
⅛ teaspoon ground nutmeg
⅓ cup chopped pecans

Bread Pudding:
1-pound loaf egg bread, crusts removed, bread cut into 1¼-inch cubes
(about 13 cups)
1 cup bittersweet chocolate chips (about 6 ounces)
1 cup chopped pecans (about 4 ounces)
4 cups whole milk
1½ cups sugar
6 large eggs
½ cup (1 stick) unsalted butter, melted, cooled
Vanilla ice cream

For praline sauce: Combine brown sugar, corn syrup, butter, brandy, cinnamon sticks, rum, vanilla extract, and nutmeg in heavy small saucepan. Bring to boil, stirring until brown sugar dissolves. Boil one minute. Mix in pecans.

Do Ahead: Sauce can be made 8 hours ahead. Let stand at room temperature. Re-warm over low heat before serving.

For Bread Pudding: Preheat oven to 350°. Butter 13x9-inch glass baking dish. Spread bread cubes in dish. Beat eggs lightly. Add milk and other ingredients. Pour over bread cubes and bake until knife inserted comes out clean. Approximately 30 to 45 minutes. Before serving, pour heated praline sauce over each individual serving and top with vanilla ice cream.

Index

Chicken

Microwave Banana Pudding   227
Bread Pudding with Warm Praline Sauce   228

Miscellaneous Desserts

Bacon — 137